THE KITE RUNNER

Khaled Hosseini

AUTHORED by Tania Asnes
UPDATED AND REVISED by W.C. Miller

COVER DESIGN by Table XI Partners LLC
COVER PHOTO by Olivia Verma and © 2005 GradeSaver, LLC

BOOK DESIGN by Table XI Partners LLC

Published by GradeSaver LLC, www.gradesaver.com

First published in the United States of America by GradeSaver LLC. 2007

GRADESAVER, the GradeSaver logo and the phrase "Getting you the grade
since 1999" are registered trademarks of GradeSaver, LLC

ISBN 978-1-60259-112-7

Printed in the United States of America

For other products and additional information please visit
http://www.gradesaver.com

Table of Contents

Table of Contents

Biography of Hosseini, Khaled (1965-)

Khaled Hosseini was born on March 4, 1965 in Kabul, the capital of Afghanistan as the oldest of five children. His father worked for the Afghan Foreign Ministry as a diplomat, and his mother was a high school teacher of Farsi and history. When he was five years old, his family moved from Kabul to Tehran, Iran. They returned to Kabul in the historic year of 1973, when Afghanistan became a republic. In 1976, his family followed his father to Paris. After the PDPA (the People's Democratic Party of Afghanistan) seized control of the government in 1978 and the Soviets occupied Afghanistan shortly thereafter, the Hosseini family decided to seek political asylum in the United States instead of returning to Kabul. They moved to San Jose, California, where Hosseini graduated from high school. He attended Santa Clara University and earned a degree in biology.

After college, Hosseini decided to become a physician. He attended the University of California-San Diego's School of Medicine, where he completed his M.D. in 1993. He served his medical residency at the well-respected Cedars-Sinai hospital of Los Angeles and became an internist. Hosseini started writing The Kite Runner in 2001 while he was a practicing physician.

Hosseini published The Kite Runner in 2003 to critical acclaim. Parts of the novel are based on Hosseini's childhood in the Kabul neighborhood of Wazir Akbar Khan. While some events in the story echo those in this life, the novel is fictional. By May 2007, it had been published in thirty-eight countries but not Afghanistan.

In 2003, while The Kite Runner was gaining a vast following, Hosseini returned to Afghanistan for the first time in twenty-seven years. He was disturbed to discover just how terrible the situation there had become, even though he had already written a very graphic fictional account of it. Hosseini has stated that a combination of luck and material privilege saved him and his family from suffering under the Soviets and the Taliban, much like his protagonist, Amir. He told *Time Magazine* that he struggled with his freedom: "I felt ashamed, like I should have suffered more." Hosseini felt estranged from the devastation in Afghanistan, but his separation from his homeland and his "Western sensibility" combined in his fiction to bring America's, and the world's, attention to the faces of Afghanistan.

Hosseini published his second novel, A Thousand Splendid Suns, in May 2007. Unlike The Kite Runner, which centers around relationships between men, A Thousand Splendid Suns focuses on those between women. In the months since its release, the novel has garnered a plethora of positive reviews.

Hosseini's devotion to Afghanistan can be seen not only in his writing but also in his activism. He has been a goodwill envoy to the United Nations Refugee Agency, UNHCR, since 2006, and his personal website contains links to many aid organizations that are helping Afghanistan. Interviewers describe Hosseini as a smart, handsome man with a calming air, and *Time Magazine* called him "almost certainly the most famous Afghan in the world." Khaled Hosseini lives with his wife and two children in Northern California.

About The Kite Runner

The Kite Runner is Khaled Hosseini's first novel. He was a practicing physician until shortly after the book's release and has now devoted himself to being an author and activist. The story of *The Kite Runner* is fictional, but it is rooted in real political and historical events ranging from the last days of the Afghan monarchy in the 1970s to the post-Taliban near present. It is also based on Hosseini's memories of growing up in the Wazir Akbar Khan section of Kabul and adapting to life in California. In a 2003 interview with *Newsline,* Hosseini specified that the most autobiographical parts of *The Kite Runner* are those about "the difficult task of assimilating into a new culture." He also revealed, "My father and I did work for a while at the flea market and there really are rows of Afghans working there, some of whom I am related to." Because Hassan did not return to Kabul until 2003, after *The Kite Runner's* publication, much of his portrayal of Afghanistan after the Soviet takeover is based on research. Hosseini's choice of time period for the book, though corresponding with his own life, also went beyond his personal experiences. He has said that he did not just want to call attention to the devastation in Afghanistan; he set out to remind the world that until the last few decades, before the world's eye was drawn to it by violence, Afghanistan was a generally peaceful nation.

Structurally, *The Kite Runner* can be divided into three sections: memories of pre-conflict Afghanistan, adjusting to life in America, and returning to Taliban-controlled Afghanistan. Thematically, it can be divided into just two: life before the rape and life after the rape. From any angle, *The Kite Runner* is a tale of love, betrayal, and redemption and it gained an enthusiastic audience from the start. After its 2003 release, *The Kite Runner* became a New York Times Bestseller and was eventually published in thirty-eight different countries, although not yet Afghanistan. Critics praised the book's intimate examination of relationships amid the fraught and very topical environment of Afghanistan. Many of them, however, expressed disappointment regarding some coincidences, specifically the way that Amir and Assef reunite. One reviewer called the moment "more suited to a folk tale" and another even deemed it worthy of a "B movie." Despite such comments, critical and popular response to *The Kite Runner* was almost universally positive.

The Kite Runner's most adoring readers and also some of its most critical are Hosseini's fellow Afghan expatriates. Hosseini said in a 2003 interview, "I get daily e-mails from Afghans who thank me for writing this book, as they feel a slice of their story has been told by one of their own. So, for the most part, I have been overwhelmed with the kindness of my fellow Afghans. There are, however, those who have called the book divisive and objected to some of the issues raised in the book, namely racism, discrimination, ethnic inequality etc." In addition to the deep feelings Hosseini's first novel aroused in the hearts of fellow Afghans, it also spurred a more lighthearted response, the resurgence of interest in kite fighting in America. The American invasion of Afghanistan may have 'put Afghanistan on the map' for Americans, but *The Kite Runner* goes farther by giving a detailed, human account of life and survival there. Its author continues this service to the world by serving as an activist in addition to writing. Hosseini has said, "If this book generates any sort of dialogue among Afghans, then I think it will have done a service to the community." As we know *The Kite Runner* has sparked conversation among Afghans and countless other groups of people worldwide. It is not such a surprise to Hosseini's admirers that a physician, accustomed to caring for people's bodies, has made such a graceful transition to caring for their histories and spirits.

Character List

Ali

Hassan's father. Ali is a Hazara whom Baba's father took in when his parents were killed. He grew up alongside Baba just as Hassan did alongside Amir. Ali has a crippled leg and paralysis in his lower face muscles and the neighborhood children ridicule him. He is as devoted and loyal as his son. Ali is killed by a land mine when Hassan is already grown.

Amir

The story's narrator and protagonist. He is an Afghan man who had a privileged childhood in the Wazir Akbar Khan neighborhood of Kabul. The defining event in his life is his betrayal of his closest friend, Hassan. Amir lives in San Francisco from the age of eighteen. He returns to Afghanistan at the age of thirty-eight and ends up adopting Hassan's orphaned son, Sohrab.

Assef

A sociopath who worships Hitler. As a child, he is the neighborhood bully who rapes Hassan. As an adult, he is a Taliban official who delights in killing people. He keeps Sohrab as a sex slave until Amir comes to rescue him. After he beats Amir nearly to death, Assef loses an eye to Sohrab's slingshot. It is possible that Hosseini based the character of Assef on the reclusive one-eyed Taliban leader, Mullah Omar.

Baba

Amir's father. He is a wealthy and well-respected man with a dark secret; he had an affair with Ali's wife and Hassan is his illegitimate son. Baba wishes Amir were braver and stronger and that he could openly express his love for Hassan. Baba dies of terminal cancer in San Francisco shortly after Amir's wedding.

Farid

The Afghan man who drives Amir from Peshawar to Kabul and ends up helping him throughout his journey. He was injured fighting against the Soviets and is fiercely proud of his loyalty to Afghanistan. He saves Amir by taking him to a hospital in Pakistan.

General Taheri

Soraya's father. He is a former general who prefers collecting welfare to lowering himself to a blue collar job. He waits every day to be called back to Afghanistan.

Hassan

Amir's most loyal and devoted servant, who is born with a clept lip. He and Amir were nursed by the same woman and, unbeknownst to them both, they are half-brothers. Hassan is illiterate but smart and stands up for others. He is also the best kite runner in Kabul. He dies at the hands of the Taliban, defending Baba's house from takeover.

Khanum Taheri

Soraya's mother. She is a kind woman who likes to sing, although her husband does not let her. She became a hypochondriac after suffering a stroke and loves Amir all the more for listening to her describe her ailments.

Omar Faisal

A lawyer who counsels Amir that his best chance is to place Sohrab in an orphanage temporarily. He was raised in America but speaks perfect Farsi.

Rahim Khan

Baba's closest friend and Amir and Hassan's confidant. He has an uncanny way of knowing what people are thinking and how to speak to them. He is one of the few people who knows Hassan's real identity and about his rape. He encourages Amir to be a writer by giving him a notebook and it is he who summons Amir back to Afghanistan to atone for his and Baba's sins.

Raymond Andrews

The official at the American Embassy who urges Amir to give up trying to rescue Sohrab. Amir thinks he is cruel and does not understand wanting a child until the secretary tells him that Raymond Andrews's daughter committed suicide.

Sanaubar

Hassan's mother. She was Ali's notoriously beautiful first cousin and second wife, who ran off with a troupe of dancers. She refused to even hold Hassan when he was born. Years later, she returns to Wazir Akbar Khan to beg forgiveness from Hassan and ends up helping raise Sohrab. She dies peacefully when he is four.

Sofia Akrami

Amir's mother, who died in childbirth. She was a professor of literature at the university and her books inspire Amir to become a writer.

Sohrab

Hassan and Farzana's son. After his parents are murdered, he stays in an orphanage in Karteh-Seh. Then he is a sex slave to Assef until Amir rescues him. Sohrab tries to commit suicide after Amir tells him he may have to stay in an orphanage again. Eventually, Amir and Soraya bring him to America and adopt him.

Soraya

Amir's wife. She shamed her family as a young woman by running off with a man. She takes care of Baba when he is ill and eagerly accepts Sohrab into her family.

Wahid

Farid's brother. When Amir stays at his house, Wahid is kind to him and does not judge him for being American. He calls Amir "a true Afghan."

Major Themes

Kites

One can tell kites are central to the novel just by reading its title, "The Kite Runner." On a plot level, the grand kite tournament of 1975 sets a circle of betrayal and redemption into motion, around which the story revolves. After Hassan gets raped while running his kite, Amir cannot separate kite fighting and running from his own betrayal and cowardice. Therefore, even after all of his injuries and trials on Sohrab's behalf, it is the act of kite running that finally makes him feel redeemed. Beyond their significance to the plot, kites have multiple layers of symbolism in the story. One of these layers involves the class difference between Amir and Hassan, which largely dictates and limits their relationship. In kite fighting, one boy controls the kite while the other assists by feeding the string. Just as Hassan makes Amir's breakfast, folds his clothes, and cleans his room, so does he cater to Amir in kite tournaments. Even though Hassan shares in the excitement of kite fighting, he does not actually have control over the kite. Hassan may help the kite "lift-and-dive," but Amir is the one who claims a victory. Hassan may catch a cherished rival kite and hold it in his arms, but always to bring it back to Amir, to whom it then belongs. His joy is vicarious, just like his experience of wealth and privilege while living in Baba's household. In order to free himself of selfishness and cowardice, Amir must go from being merely a kite fighter-someone who seeks glory-to a kite runner, someone who genuinely does things for others.

The activity of kite fighting is violent by nature. The kites battle and so too do the children flying them. The string, which is covered in ground glass, carves deep gashes into the fliers' hands as they try to cut each other down, and once kites fall out of the sky, the kite runners retrieve them with the same furious determination as, say, a hunting dog does a slain bird. In its violence, kite fighting represents the conflicts that rage Afghanistan nearly throughout the course of the novel. When Hosseini paints us a picture of hundreds of kites trying haphazardly and with great determination to cut each other down, he shows us also the warring factions of Afghanistan overthrowing one another. At the same time kite fighting is violent, the mere act of kite flying is innocent and speaks of freedom. Amir and Hassan do not have control over the differences between them; in fact, they are both the victims of a lie, and their relationship would have been different had they known they were brothers. Yet despite their differences and the symbolism of their respective kite-fighting roles, flying kites is an activity that brings the boys together. For a moment, they are part of a team. For many years, Amir feels as though he and Hassan are adversaries for Baba's love. After the rape, Hassan's very existence infuriates Amir because it reminds him of his cowardice. Despite all this, when the boys fly kites together, they are on the same team. They are more like brothers then than perhaps any other time, because the activity is somewhat mutual. It allows them to momentarily escape their differences and enjoy a shared sense of exhilaration and freedom. The cover of *The Kite Runner* shows a kite flying very high over Kabul. This image can be seen to represent Amir and Hassan's shared sense of freedom, one that takes them away from life's realities until the kite is grounded again.

Discrimination

The Kite Runner tackles the issue of ethnic discrimination in Afghanistan with an example of the relationship between Pashtuns and Hazaras. Baba's father sets an example for him of being kind to Hazara people, even though they are historically demeaned and persecuted. He could have easily sent Ali to an orphanage after his parents' death, but chose to raise him in his household. Baba does the same with Hassan, although this is complicated by the fact that Hassan is actually his son. Even in Baba's house, the house of best intentions, the class barrier between the Pashtuns and Hazaras endures. Ali is as dear to Baba as a brother; he calls him "family." But Ali still lives in a hut and sleeps on a mattress on the floor. He tends the garden, cooks, and cleans up after Baba, and raises Hassan to do the same. So strong is Hassan's identity as a servant that even as an adult, when Baba is gone, he has no sense of entitlement. He insists on staying in the hut and doing housework. When Hassan dies defending Baba's house, he does so not because he feels it belongs to him, but because he is being loyal to Baba and Amir.

In Taliban-controlled Afghanistan, discrimination is everywhere and nowhere at the same time. On the one hand, the Taliban do not seem to care whom they are beating, torturing, or executing. Children like Sohrab and grandmothers like Sanaubar are all susceptible to the Taliban's cruelty. In this way, the Talibs discriminate against everyone but themselves. As Amir notices, Assef forces Sohrab to dance to music for his enjoyment dancing and listening to music have long been banned. Amir thinks, "I guessed music wasn't sinful as long as it played to Taliban ears." On another level, the Taliban discriminate specifically against the Hazara people. They massacre the Hazaras not only in Mazar-i-Sharif, but in the region of Hazarajat and nearly anywhere else they can find them. Assef and his fellows do not see the Hazaras' lives as worthwhile; they barely see them as human. Assef tells Amir, "Afghanistan is like a beautiful mansion littered with garbage, and someone has to take out the garbage." Like his idol, Hitler, he feels entitled to killing those he deems unworthy of living in his land. He even relishes the term "ethnic cleansing" because it goes so well with his garbage metaphor. Hosseini has mentioned in interviews that his focus on discrimination in *The Kite Runner* angers some Afghans, who feel it is inappropriate. Like Baba, many people do not mention the Hazaras' history of persecution. Perhaps these people are so uncomfortable with this topic because by having Assef appear in pre-Taliban times and emerge as a leading Talib, Hosseini shows that the Taliban's persecution of the Hazaras and other Shiites is not new, but a greatly intensified outgrowth of long-held discrimination.

Sin and Redemption

In *The Kite Runner,* redemption is so important because sin is so enduring. Amir opens the story by telling us not about how exactly he sinned, but about sin's endurance: "... It's wrong what they say about the past, I've learned, about how you can bury it. Because the past claws its way out." Hosseini uses structure to emphasize the themes of sin and redemption. Because Amir tells the story in retrospect, every memory, even the blissful ones of his childhood before the rape, are tainted with it. If the timeline of the novel was strictly chronological, we would not have the power of hindsight. Hosseini uses the first chapter almost like a thesis for the novel. As Amir retells the story of his life, he weighs each event against his sin, his betrayal of Hassan. As we learn towards the novel's end, Amir is not the only character who needs redemption, Assef notwithstanding. Until Rahim Khan reveals Baba's secret, Amir thinks he is the only sinner among his family and friends. Even before Amir betrays him, Hassan makes him feel guilty simply by being such a righteous person. Amir is constantly trying to measure up to Baba, because he does not realize that Baba is so hard on him because of his guilt over his own sin.

One Amir finds out about Baba's sin, he feels as though his entire life has been a cycle of betrayal, even before he betrayed Hassan. But having a taste of betrayal himself does little towards redeeming Amir. In Ghazi Stadium, the Taliban skews the words of Muhammad in order to justify murdering the alleged adulterers. The mullah announces that every person should have a punishment befitting his sin. Although he would not want to compare himself to the Taliban, Amir believes this in regards to his own sin. When he tries to get Hassan to pelt him with pomegranates, he is expressing his feeling that in order to be forgiven for hurting Hassan, Hassan must hurt him. When Assef almost kills Amir, he feels "healed," as though now that Assef has hurt him, he is redeemed. He even tells Farid that in the room with Assef, he "got what he deserved." In the end, Amir finds out that punishment is not what will redeem him from his sin. It is not even saving Sohrab. In order to atone for his sin and Baba's before him, Amir must erase the lines of discrimination he has lived with all his life by giving Sohrab an equal chance at success and happiness.

Soraya needs Amir to forgive her before she can marry him. In the same way, Rahim Khan needs Amir to forgive him for keeping Baba's secret before he dies. Rahim Khan, the story's unofficial wise man, is the one who truly understands how redemption occurs. He tells Amir in his letter, "I know that in the end, God will forgive. He will forgive your father, me, and you too ... Forgive your father if you can. Forgive me if you wish. But most important, forgive yourself." Rahim Khan carries the novel's ultimate message about forgiveness. God is merciful; it is people who are not. Therefore, truly atoning for one's sins means coming to terms with them by oneself, without relying on a higher power. When Amir prays, he is still bound by fear and guilt; instead of wishing unselfishly for Sohrab to recover, he begs God not to leave "Sohrab's blood on his hands." When Amir manages to forgive himself in the very last moments of the novel, he redeems himself at last.

Literacy and the Written Word

In the novel, writing is both a dividing force and a uniting one. Amir's wish to be a writer separates him from Baba, who wants him to be athletic and equates his bookishness with weakness. In Amir's young life, his ability to read and write separates him from Hassan. Because Hassan is a Hazara and expected to remain a servant like Ali before him, no one makes sure he is literate. While Amir goes to school every day, Hassan stays behind and does his chores. On the one hand, Hassan's illiteracy brings him closer to Amir. The boys spend countless hours together under the pomegranate tree, Amir reading stories to Hassan. When Amir begins to write stories, Hassan is his rapt audience. Yet Amir realizes that being literate gives him power over Hassan. He lords his advantage over the unsuspecting Hassan by making up stories while pretending to read and teasing Hassan for not knowing certain words. Only later does Hassan realize the power of literacy and its connection to social power. He makes sure that Sohrab can read and write and expresses his wish for Sohrab to be "someone important."

Despite the connection between literacy and discrimination, the written word is largely a unifying force in the novel. One thing that makes Amir admire Soraya even more is her story of how she taught an illiterate woman to read and write. That act of teaching unified Soraya and the woman; the telling of it brings her and Amir closer together. Traditionally, the power of the written word is located in its endurance beyond death. This rings true in the novel when Amir reads Hassan's letter, although as he reads it he does not yet know Hassan is dead. Additionally remarkable about Hassan's letter is that it puts him on an equal level with Hassan; now that he is literate, written words are no longer a barrier between them. Rahim Khan's letter is the final one in the novel, and it is also the one containing the ultimate message about forgiveness. Hosseini gives extra emphasis to writing's importance by putting this central message in written form.

Family Ties

Family is extremely important in the story, especially because it takes place in Afghanistan. It is a nation where culture and tradition are of monumental importance, especially to the older generation. We see this when Baba and Amir are in America. Even though they are in a different country, Amir is expected to observe cultural tradition in courting Soraya. Not only must they go through *khastegari,* in order to get engaged, but they cannot be seen together in public before the wedding. One the one hand, everyone in Afghanistan is part of one family; as Baba says, "Take two Afghans who've never met, put them in a room for ten minutes, and they'll figure out how they're related." On the other hand, lineage is of the utmost importance. When Amir and Soraya are condisering adopting a child, General Taheri explains that Afghans are not meant to disturb their family line with such a decision. He tells them that Baba's reputation was a big consideration in regards to their marriage and says, "Blood is a powerful thing ... And when you adopt, you don't know whose blood you're bringing into your house."

What General Taheri does not know is that for the very reason that family is so important to Afghans, Baba kept Hassan's identity secret to his grave. To him, denying Hassan his identity was preferable to confusing the relationship between Ali and himself and that between Amir and Hassan. Baba treats Ali and Hassan as equally as he felt he could without destroying his and Ali's honor, but Baba knows that they are his family. Amir does not have this privilege and his ignorance makes him more irreverent towards Hassan, who is loyal as a brother to him anyway. Family is more important to Amir than he knows; his guilt over hurting Hassan is terrible when he thinks Hassan is just another person. Once he knows they are related, he is overcome with guilt, enough to put himself in danger and stand up for Sohrab. For much of his life, Amir feels as though his family is the cause of his problems. He thinks Baba blames him for his mother's death and spends much of his childhood tormented by trying to win a place in Baba's heart. Family is the reason why Amir fights to bring Sohrab home and, ultimately, the channel through which he redeems himself.

Violence

Even though Hosseini has stated that he wanted to remind people of a peaceful Afghanistan, he also does the service of revealing the suffering the nation has experienced in a quarter century of conflict. Violence pervades the novel, even in the seemingly innocuous activity of kite fighting. Not only is kite fighting violent because it is a kind of battle, but boys injure their hands when they participate. This fact suggests that Afghanistan has become a place where joy cannot exist separately from pain; Afghans' memories of their homeland are tainted with suffering. The entire novel centers around a single act of violence, Hassan's rape, and the sin Amir commits by pretending that violence did not occur. Symbolically, Hassan's rape is echoed by Sohrab's rape decades later and by Afghanistan's continual rape by war and terrorism.

Amir's life in America does involve suffering, especially regarding Baba's death. But Baba's death is peaceful. Because America is a haven from violence, the violence under the Taliban in Kabul is even more shocking and sobering. Amir gets a taste of violence when he and Baba are fleeing for Pakistan and Kamal's father commits suicide. However, nothing can prepare him for the extent of violence and suffering in Afghanistann. One of the most graphic accounts is of the stonings at Ghazi Stadium. Like the rapes of Hassan and Sohrab, the event symbolizes the devastation of Afghanistan as a whole, as Afghans once knew it. Anothr very violent event is Amir's fight with Assef. At the time, Amir's pain makes him feel happy and "healed"; it is as though by suffering, he is repaying Hassan for all the violence he suffered on Amir's behalf. Amir's split lip, though minor compared to his other injuries, is most significant because it represents this feeling of closeness to Hassan. Yet we learn that violence is not the answer to Amir's problems, nor does he understand just how deep its consequences run. When young Sohrab tries to kill himself, Amir sees that his nearly fatal injuries were nothing compared to the pain Sohrab and other Afghans have suffered.

Ultimately, he finds out that the only way to heal the violence done to Hassan and Sohrab is to forgive himself.

Homeland and Nationality

Because Amir immigrates to the United States when he is still growing up, the question of his national identity is especially complex. Baba sees America as a refuge and becomes enthralled, as Amir says, with "the *idea* of America." He identifies with American optimism and freedom of choice, and even hangs a framed picture of Ronald Reagan on the wall of their apartment. Up until his death, Baba is a guest in America; Afghanistan is undeniably the place where he can be himself. There, he was a successful and influential figure. In America, he must work at the gas station and suffer the humiliation of being a foreigner, as with the Nguyens. For young Amir, America is not only politically free, but more importantly, free of Hassan and memories of him. He uses the image of a river to describe the exhilaration and cleansing effect that being in America has on him. He opens his arms wide to America, even though he maintains Afghan traditions regarding courtship and writes a novel about Afghanistan. Because he comes into adulthood in America, Amir does not suffer along with his fellow Afghans. As he discovers, this makes all the difference in defining his national identity.

Amir's coming to Afghanistan should by all accounts be a homecoming, but Amir can never truly revisit his homeland; it no longer exists as he knew it. In the interim between Amir's flight from Kabul and his return, the Soviets, warring factions, and the Taliban have turned it from a culturally rich and bustling place into a ghost town of beggars among the rubble and hanging corpses. Amir can no longer be an Afghan because being an Afghan has become synonymous with having survived terror, if not much worse. According to Farid, however, Amir never had an Afghan identity to lose. He tells Amir that his privileged upbringing has made him a "tourist" in Afghanistan all his life. Amir himself tells Rahim Khan that he cannot go to Afghanistan because he has a wife, a home, and a life in America. Through these conversations, Hosseini asks what constitutes a homeland, a *watan*. If Farid is right, then Amir has no homeland. However, once Farid finds out why Amir has returned to Afghanistan, he changes his opinion of him. He seems to accept him as a friend, if not a countryman. According to the novel, then, one's homeland depends not only on one's emotional attachment to a place but one's tangible devotion to it. To make a place one's homeland, Hosseini seems to suggest, one must be willing not merely to dwell on nostalgic feelings but to put them into action-whether like Farid, by fighting in a trench, or like Amir, by trying to save someone from the homeland itself.

Glossary of Terms

Hazara

A term describing the Hazara people, an ethnic minority originating in the mountainous region of Afghanistan called Hazarajat. Characterized by their mongoloid facial features, adherence to Shi'a Islam, and long history of persecution.

hypochondriac

One who is consistently and habitually convinced he is ill when he is not.

INS

Immigration and Nationalization Service of the United States of America. Formerly, the government agency that oversaw immigration issues. Now the United States Citizenship and Immigration Services.

Mazar-i-Sharif

A large city in Afghanistan famous for its Blue Mosque. The Taliban massacred the Hazara population there in 1998.

Mujahedin

A term used to describe a group of Muslims engaged in a war or conflict. In this novel, it describes the Afghanistan Mujahedin Freedom Fighters Front, which challenged the Soviet forces and later lost against the PDPA (People's Democratic Party of Afghanistan) government.

Pashtun

An ethnic group forming a majority in Afghanistan and surrounding areas. Characterized by adherence to Sunni Islam as well as Pashtunwali, an ancient code of tradition.

Shi'a Islam

The second largest denomination of the Islamic faith. Shi'a Islam believes that the teachings of Muhammad were carried through his descendants and do not accept the caliphate.

Shorawi

The Farsi term for the Soviets, who invaded Afghanistan in 1979 and occupied the country for a decade.

Sunni Islam

The largest denomination of Islam. Sunni Islam accepts the caliphate, meaning that it considers the Caliph or head of a Muslim state a successor to Muhammad.

Wazir Akbar Khan

The neighborhood in Kabul where Amir and Hassan grew up.

Short Summary

The story is narrated from the year 2002. Amir, who is thus far a nameless protagonist, tells us that an event in the winter of 1975 changed his life forever. We do not know anything about this event except that it still haunts him and that it involves something he did to Hassan, whom he calls "the harelipped kite runner." Amir takes us back to his childhood, in the final decades of the monarchy in Afghanistan. His father, Baba, was one of the wealthiest and most charitable Pashtun men in Kabul, where they lived in the Wazir Akbar Khan neighborhood. His mother died in childbirth. Amir's closest friend, the harelipped Hassan, was also his servant and a Hazara. He was very close to his father, Ali, who was Baba's servant.

Despite their differences, Amir and Hassan were inseparable. Hassan would have done anything for Amir; his first word was even "Amir." Baba was aloof and did not pay Amir much attention. He was a huge and imposing man who was rumored to have wrestled a bear. Baba did not subscribe to popular belief, preferring to cast his own opinions about issues. Baba wished Amir was athletic and brave like him instead of cowardly and bookish.

Amir explains how Ali and Baba knew each other. Baba's father took Ali into his house after Ali's parents were killed in an accident. Ali and Baba grew up together just like Hassan and Amir. In each generation, the boys could never truly consider themselves friends because of their class differences. One big difference divider was literacy. Amir was proud of his literacy and lorded it over the unsuspecting, illiterate Hassan. Yet when Amir wrote his first short story and read it to Hassan, it was the latter who found the plot hole in the story.

That same night, July 17, 1973, there was a coup d'etat in Afghanistan, changing it from a monarchy to a republic. Unbeknownst to the boys or anyone else, it was the first of many political changes that would eventually ruin Afghanistan as they knew it. One day, Amir and Hassan got into a confrontation with a boy named Assef and his two friends. Assef idolized Hitler and hated Hazaras. As usual, Hassan stood up for Amir; he got Assef to leave by aiming his slingshot at Assef's eye. That same year, Baba got Hassan surgery to fix his harelip.

In the winter, schools were closed in Kabul and the boys spent much time kite fighting. When defeated kites fell out of the sky, boys chased them to try to bring them home as trophies. They were called "kite runners." Amir usually flew a kite while Hassan ran kites for him. Hassan was the best kite runner anyone had ever seen. He had an innate sense of where a kite would land.

In the winter of 1975, there was a massive kite tournament. Amazingly, Amir won, and Hassan went to run the last kite for him. Before he chased it, he shouted, "For you, a thousand times over." When Hassan did not come home, Amir went out looking for him. He found Hassan confronting Assef and his two friends in an alley.

Amir did nothing to help Hassan as Assef raped him. Later he found Hassan walking home, kite in hand, with blood dripping from his pants. He pretended not to know what happened and did not tell Ali the truth when he asked.

After the kite tournament, Amir's relationship with his father improved because Baba was so proud of him. His relationship with Hassan degraded. Amir was too ashamed of what he had done to face Hassan and avoided him at all costs. One day he even suggested to Baba that they get new servants. To his surprise, Baba was furious and threatened to hit Amir for the first time. He said that Ali and Hassan were their family. Amir tried to resolve his guilt by teaching Hassan not to be so loyal to him. He took Hassan up to the hill and pelted him with pomegranates. No matter how much he begged, Hassan would not hit him back. Hassan smashed a pomegranate into his own forehead and asked Amir if he felt better.

Amir's guilt intensified at the lavish thirteenth birthday party that Baba threw for him. He knew Baba never would have given him such a great party had he not won the tournament, which was inseparable in his mind from Hassan's rape. Assef came to the party and gave Amir a book about Hitler. Amir was disgusted to see him teasing Hassan during the party. Baba gave Amir a wristwatch. Rahim Khan gave him the only present he could bear to use, which was a blank notebook for his stories. He also received a good deal of money. To his chagrin, Ali and Hassan gave him a copy of his and Hassan's favorite book. After the party, Amir decided to betray Hassan a second time and frame him as a thief. He hid his wristwatch and money under Hassan and Ali's mattress. The next morning, he accused Hassan, who took the blame as usual. Baba forgave him immediately, but Hassan and Ali were too humiliated to stay. As they left, Amir saw Baba weep for the first time. They never saw Ali or Hassan again.

Five years later, during the Soviet occupation, Amir and Baba fled Afghanistan in a truck full of refugees. When they reached a checkpoint, a Russian soldier demanded to sleep with one of them, a married woman. Baba stood up for her even though the soldier was armed. They were allowed to pass. After hiding in a basement in Jalalabad, they departed for Peshawar, Pakistan in the filthy tank of a fuel truck. Among the refugees were Amir's schoolmate, Kamal, and his father. When they arrived, they discovered that Kamal was dead. Kamal's father put a gun in his mouth and shot himself. Luckily, Amir and Baba managed to emigrate to the San Francisco area.

Baba and Amir's life in Fremont, California was very different from their life in Wazir Akbar Khan. Baba worked long hours at a gas station and even though he loved "the *idea* of America," had trouble adjusting to its everyday realities. For Amir, America represented a fresh beginning, free of all his haunting memories of Hassan. He graduated high school at the age of twenty and planned to enroll in junior college. His graduation gave Baba a reason to celebrate, but he said he wished Hassan were with them. Eventually, Baba and Amir started selling used goods at a local flea market. They found it to be a miniature Afghan haven, filled with people they knew from Kabul.

At the flea market, Amir fell in love with a young woman named Soraya Taheri. Around the same time, Baba got sick. A doctor diagnosed Baba with terminal cancer and Baba refused palliative treatments. Then one day Baba collapsed with seizures in the flea market; the cancer had spread to his brain and he did not have long to live. Very soon after, Amir asked Baba to go *khastegari*, to ask for Soraya's hand in marriage. The Taheris accepted happily. Over the phone, Soraya told Amir her shameful secret. She had once run away with an Afghan man. When General Taheri finally forced her to come home, she had to cut off all her hair in shame. Amir told Soraya he still wanted to marry her. He felt ashamed that he could not bring himself to tell her his secret in return.

After *khastegari* came *lafz*, "the ceremony of giving word." Because Baba was so ill, Soraya and Amir decided to forgo the *Shirini-kori*, the traditional engagement party, as well as the engagement period. Baba spent almost all his money on the *awroussi*, the wedding ceremony. Soraya moved in with Amir and Baba so they could spend his last days together. She took care of him until the night he died peacefully in his sleep.

Many people attended Baba's funeral, each with a story of how Baba had helped them in Afghanistan. Suddenly, Amir realized that he had formed his identity around being "Baba's son." Amir and Soraya moved into their own apartment and worked towards their college degrees. In 1988, Amir published his first novel. Around the same time, the Soviets withdrew from Afghanistan, but new conflicts erupted. Soon after, the Cold War ended, the Berlin Wall fell, and the riots occurred in Tiananmen Square. In San Francisco, Amir and Soraya bought a house and discovered they were infertile. There was no medical explanation for the infertility, so Amir privately blamed it on his own shameful past.

One day, Amir received a call from Rahim Khan. He was seriously ill and was living in Peshawar. He told Amir, "There is a way to be good again." Amir flew to Peshawar to see Rahim Khan, who told him that he was dying. He explained that the Taliban had destroyed Afghanistan as they knew it and the people there were in grave danger. For a chapter, Rahim Khan becomes the narrator and tells Amir about what happened to Hassan. For a long time, Rahim Khan had lived in Baba's house alone, but he became weak and lonely. In 1986 he went looking for Hassan and found him living in a small village with his pregnant wife, Farzana. Hassan did not want to come to Wazir Akbar Khan until Rahim Khan told him about Baba's death. Hassan cried all night and in the morning, he and Farzana moved in with Rahim Khan.

Hassan and Farzana insisted on staying in the servants' hut and doing housework. Farzana's first baby was stillborn. One day, Sanaubar collapsed at the gate of the house. She had traveled a long way to finally make peace with Hassan, who accepted her with open arms. Sanaubar delivered Hassan and Farzana's son, Sohrab and played a large part in raising him. She died when he was four. Hassan made sure that Sohrab was loved, literate, and great with a slingshot. When the Taliban took over in 1996, people celebrated, but Hassan predicted that things would get worse, as they did. In 198, the Taliban massacred the Hazaras in Mazar-i-Sharif.

Rahim Khan gave Amir a letter that Hassan had written six months earlier along with a snapshot of him and Sohrab. In the letter, Hassan described the terror of living under the Taliban. He said he hoped Amir would return to Afghanistan and that they would reunite. Then Rahim Khan devastated Amir with the news that Hassan was dead. After Rahim Khan left to seek medical treatment in Pakistan, the Taliban showed up at Baba's house. They demanded that Hassan relinquish the house to them. When he refused, they took him to the street, made him kneel, and shot him in the back of the head. They shot Farzana too when she ran out of the house in a rage.

Rahim Khan asked Amir to go to Kabul and bring Sohrab back to Peshawar. He said that a nice American couple, the Caldwells, had a goodwill organization and would take care of him there. When Amir refused, Rahim Khan told him a life-changing secret: he and Hassan were half-brothers. Baba had shamed Ali by sleeping with Sanaubar, and because Ali was infertile, Hassan had to be Baba's son. Amir flew into a rage and ran out of Rahim Khan's apartment. After thinking things over at a cafÃ©, he returned and said he would bring Sohrab to Peshawar.

A driver named Farid drove Amir from Peshawar. He looked down on Amir for leaving Afghanistan because he had stayed to fight the Soviets and suffered along with his country. He even told Amir that he had never been a real Afghan because he grew up with so many privileges. Amir did feel like a foreigner because he had to wear a fake beard and was dressed in traditional Afghan clothing for the first time. He barely recognized the landscape around him because it was so ravaged by war. They spent the night with Farid's brother, Wahid. Wahid's boys were malnourished and later that night, Amir heard one of his two wives complaining that he had given all the food to their guests. The next morning, Amir hid money under Wahid's mattress before they left.

The devastation in Kabul took Amir's breath away. Children and mothers begged on every street corner, and there were few men to be seen because so many had died fighting. Amir met an old beggar who was once a professor at the university alongside Amir's mother. Amir learns only a few random facts about his mother from the man, but this is still more than Baba ever told him. At the orphanage in Karteh-Seh, Farid and Amir discovered that a Talib official who was a pedophile had taken Sohrab a month before. Farid was so enranged at the man that he tried to strangle him to death, but Amir intervened. The man told them they could find the Talib at Ghazi Stadium. Farid drove Amir to Baba's house, which had become decrepit and was occupied by the Taliban. He and Farid spent the night in a run-down hotel.

Farid and Amir went to a soccer game at Ghazi Stadium. At halftime, the Talibs brought two accused adulterers out to the field and made them stand in pits in the ground. Then the Talib official came out and stoned them to death. Amir managed to make an appointment with this Talib for the same day. Farid drove him there, but Amir went in alone. The Talib had his men rip off Amir's fake beard. Then he called in Sohrab and made him dance for them. Sohrab looked terrified. Amir was horrified to discover that the Talib was Assef. Assef explained that he was on a mission to kill all the Hazaras in Afghanistan. Then he announced that he and Amir would fight to the death and none of his guards were to intervene. Sohrab was made to watch as Assef beat Amir nearly to death. As Assef straddled Amir, preparing to punch him again, Sohrab aimed his slingshot at Assef's eye and begged him to stop. When he did not, Sohrab put out his eye. Farid drove them away and Amir passed out.

Amir flitted in and out of consciousness in the Pakistani hospital where Farid took him. He dreamed about Baba fighting the bear, and realized that he was Baba. When he finally came to, he found out that he had almost died of a ruptured spleen. He had broken his ribs and a bone in his face and he had a punctured lung, among other injuries. Most poignantly, Amir's lip had split open to make him resemble Hassan. Sohrab visited Amir in the hospital but did not talk much. Farid brought a letter and a key from Rahim Khan. In the letter, Rahim urged Amir to forgive himself for what he did to Hassan. He had left Amir money in a safety deposit box, which the key would open.

Amir had to leave the hospital early in order to avoid being found and killed by Taliban sympathizers. He and Sohrab stayed at a hotel in Islamabad. The first night, Amir woke up to find Sohrab gone. After hours of searching he found him staring up at the city's big Shah Faisal mosque. Sohrab revealed that he was afraid God would punish him for what he did to Assef. He felt dirty and sinful from being abused. Amir tried to reassure him and promised to take him to America. He also promised Sohrab that he would never have to go to another orphanage. That night, Amir spoke to Soraya. After all their years of marriage, he finally told her what he did to Hassan. Then told her he was bringing Sohrab home. Soraya was very supportive and promised to call her cousin Sharif, who worked for the INS.

At the American Embassy, an official named Raymond Andrews told Amir that it would be near impossible to get Sohrab a visa. To Amir's disgust, he told him to give up. Then a kind lawyer named Omar Faisal told Amir that he might have a chance of adopting Sohrab if he put him in an orphanage temporarily. When Amir told Sohrab about the orphanage, the boy was devastated. Amir rocked him to sleep and fell asleep as well. Soraya's call woke Amir. She explained that Sharif would be able to get Sohrab a visa. Realizing Sohrab was in the bath, Amir went in to tell him the good news. He found him dying in the bathtub, having slit his wrists.

In the hospital waiting for news about Sohrab, Amir prayed for the first time in fifteen years. He begged God to let Sohrab live because he did not want his blood on his hands. Eventually, he received the good news that Sohrab was alive.

The story jumps to the present year, 2002. Sohrab and Amir were able to come back to America safely. It had now been a year since they arrived and Sohrab had not spoken once. He barely seemed to have a will to live. Amir kept Sohrab's past secret from the Taheris until General Taheri called him a "Hazara boy." Amir was furious; he told the general never to refer to Amir that way again. Then he explained that Sohrab was his illegitimate half-nephew. General Taheri stopped asking questions after that. After September 11, General Taheri was called back to Afghanistan. In the wake of what happened, Amir found it strange to hear people on the news and on the street talking about the cities of his childhood. It saddened him to know that his country was still beind devastated after so many decades of violence. Then one day, a miracle happened.

At a rainy Afghan picnic, Amir noticed kites flying in the sky. He bought one and went over to Sohrab, who had secluded himself as usual. He told Sohrab that Hassan was the best kite runner he had ever known and asked Sohrab if he wanted to fly the kite. Sohrab was shy, but he followed Amir as he launched the kite into the air. Soon after, they noticed a green kite closing in on theirs. Amir used Hassan's favorite "lift-and-dive" move to cut the kite. Amir noticed the smallest hint of a smile on Sohrab's face. He offered to run the kite for Sohrab and as he ran off, he shouted, "For you, a thousand times over."

Summary and Analysis of Chapters 1-3

Summary

Chapter One

The Kite Runner begins with our thus-far nameless protagonist explaining that the past cannot be forgotten. A single moment in time defined him and has been affecting him for the last twenty-six years. This moment was in 1975 when he was twelve years old and hid near a crumbling alleyway in his hometown of Kabul, Afghanistan. When the protagonist's friend, Rahim Khan, calls him out of the blue, he knows that his past sins are coming back to haunt him even in the new life he has built in San Francisco. He remembers Hassan, whom he calls "the harelipped kite runner," saying "For you, a thousand times over." Rahim's words also echo in his head, "There is a way to be good again." These two phrases will become focal points for the rest of the novel and our protagonist's story.

Chapter Two

The protagonist remembers sitting in trees with Hassan when they were boys and annoying the neighbors. Any mischief they perpetrated was the protagonist's idea, but even when Hassan's father, Ali, scolded Hassan, he never told on the protagonist. Hassan's father was a servant to the protagonist's father, Baba and lived in a small servant's house on his property. Baba's house was widely considered the most beautiful one in Kabul. There Baba held large dinner parties and entertained friends, including Rahim Khan, in his smoking room. Though the protagonist was often surrounded by adults, he never knew his mother because she died in childbirth. Hassan never knew his mother, either, because she eloped with a performance troupe a few days after his birth. The protagonist always felt a special affinity with Hassan because he too was motherless. It was not a surprise that Hassan's mother, Sanaubar, left Ali. The only things these first cousins had in common were being of the Hazara ethnicity and the Shi'a religion. Otherwise, Sanaubar was nineteen years younger than Ali, gorgeous, and reportedly promiscuous. Meanwhile Ali was a pious man afflicted by paralysis of the lower face muscles and a crippled leg. Rumor had it that Sanaubar taunted Ali for his disabilities just as cruelly as strangers and refused to even hold the infant Hassan because of his cleft lip.

One night, after hearing so many insults thrown at Hassan because he was Hazara, the protagonist secretly read a summary of Hazara history. He found out that the Hazara people were descended from Moguls, owing to their flattened, "Chinese-like" facial features. The Hazaras were brutally oppressed throughout their history for being Shi'a instead of Sunni Muslim. His own people, the Pashtun, oppressed the Hazaras. The protagonist wondered why Baba had never told him any of this. He pitied Hassan for being a hated minority because he was an unusually gentle and kind person, "incapable of hurting anyone." In lieu of the boys' mothers, a kindly woman nursed and sang to both of them. Ali used to remind the boys that they were bound together because they had "fed from the same breasts." The boys were indeed like brothers. The protagonist explains that his first word was "Baba" while Hassan's was his name, "Amir." He says that the event that transpired in 1975, to which he alluded in Chapter One, was "already laid in those first words."

Chapter Three

Amir describes Baba as being a huge and intimidating man who stood six feet, five inches tall and was purported to have wrestled a bear because of the long scars on his back. Despite his huge size, Baba was softhearted. He even devoted three years to funding and building an orphanage. Amir was proud to have such a successful father. Together with Rahim Khan, Baba owned several successful businesses and he had also married well; Amir's mother, Sofia Akrami, was a highly respected and educated poetry professor of royal descent. However, Baba's successes took him away from home and from Amir most of the time. When he was present, he was usually aloof.

One day in school, a Mullah or Muslim teacher told Amir and his classmates that drinking was a sin. When he got home, Amir asked Baba, a frequent drinker, about what the teacher had said. Baba told Amir that ultra religious people were not only wrong in their convictions but dangerous. He said, prophetically, "God help us all if Afghanistan ever falls into their hands." Then he explained to Amir that the only sin is stealing, whether a piece of property or a life. Baba knew about having things stolen firsthand; his father's life was stolen by a thief who stabbed him to death while robbing his house. Amir was grateful that Baba spoke to him so personally, but felt a simultaneous guilt for not being more like his father. He always felt that Baba hated him a little for 'killing' his mother as he was born.

Because Baba was aloof and often absent, Amir turned his attention to books. By the age of eleven, he could recite more poetry than anyone in his class at school. Baba wanted Amir to be an athlete like him, but Amir was not talented at soccer and did not have an interest in Baba's choice sport. Once, Baba took Amir to the yearly Buzkashi tournament. Buzkashi is a traditional Afghani sport in which a "highly skilled horseman" called a chapandaz from one team must retrieve an animal carcass from inside the other team's stampede and drop it in a special scoring circle while being chased by chapandaz from the other team who try to steal the carcass from him. As they sat watching the tournament, Baba pointed out Henry Kissinger, who was sitting in the bleachers, to Amir. Before Amir had a chance to ask Baba who Henry Kissinger was, one chapandaz fell off his horse and was trampled to death. Amir cried all the way home while Baba tried unsuccessfully to hide his disgust at his son's weak disposition. Back at home, Amir overheard Baba complaining to Rahim Khan about how Amir was always lost in his books and did not stand up for himself. Rahim Khan told Baba that he was self-centered, but Baba maintained that Amir was "missing something." Amir heard him say, "If I hadn't seen the doctor pull him out of my wife with my own eyes, I'd never believe he's my son."

Analysis

Though brief, Chapter One of *The Kite Runner* sets the tone for the entire novel. Before we know anything about the protagonist, including his name, we learn that one moment in his past has defined his entire life. We do not learn exactly what the moment is until Chapter Seven. This tells us that the event has significance beyond its detail; it is not so much specifically the rape, but more generally the betrayal, that makes that moment in time so central to Amir's life. We also discover in the short first chapter that Amir has been trying to forget his secret for the last twenty-six years. His betrayal of Hassan haunts him continually throughout his life, but it is not until he is 'caught' that it spurs him to action-and then, very reluctantly. When Amir thinks he is alone with his secret, he can pretend it does not exist. Once he finds out that Rahim Khan knows what he did, he cannot hide from it anymore. Khaled Hosseini makes extensive use of foreshadowing in *The Kite Runner,* including Baba's statement, "God help us all if Afghanistan ever falls into [the religious fundamentalists'] hands," which anticipates the Taliban's takeover decades later. Hosseini's use of foreshadowing connects him to the genre of magical realism. Even though there are no supernatural events in the novel, there is an underlying sense that every action has significance and must come full circle.

From the foreshadowing in Chapter One, we can surmise that Amir's guilt has something to do with Hassan. That an event involving Hassan has defined Amir's entire life indicates Hassan's monumental importance as a character. Amir feels powerless as a child, so he takes out his frustrations on his unsuspecting best friend. He lords his privileges and his education over Hassan, but in reality it is Hassan who has power over him. We can tell this even from the title, which refers to Hassan (though also to Amir at the story's end). The most obvious indicator of Hassan's importance is the fact that Amir does not mention his own name until he reveals that it was Hassan's first word. It is as though Amir as we know him does not exist without Hassan, as though Hassan's voice-representing his influence-made Amir come into being.

The theme of loyalty is central to the novel. Amir's lack of loyalty to Hassan is what keeps him rooted to that one moment in the winter of 1975. Hassan's unflinching loyalty to Amir is what results in his rape, his leaving Wazir Akhbar Khan, and one could argue, his death many years later. We learn the basics of Amir and Hassan's relationship early on, as embodied in their mischief making. Amir is a child of privilege who wants attention, so he feels safe and even entitled to getting into trouble. Yet his insecurity and fear of Baba makes him unable to stand up for himself or take credit for his mistakes. In contrast, Hassan is a servant who has a very close and constant relationship with his father, Ali. Ali has taught Hassan to be so righteous and loyal that he would not dream of starting trouble and does not hesitate to cover up for Amir. As we learn, Hassan is so determined to protect Amir and not to cause anyone grief that he keeps his rape a secret. The difference between Amir and Hassan underscores the connection between loyalty and family. Hassan is loyal and long-suffering just like Ali, who kept the secret that Baba had an affair with

Sanaubar and that Hassan was not his biological son. Amir betrays Hassan just as Baba betrayed Ali, and like Baba, Amir must suffer for what he did and pay retribution.

The theme of loyalty is connected to the theme of silence and secrets. Remaining silent about injustice is Ali and Hassan's way of showing loyalty to Baba and Amir. The story of *The Kite Runner* is filled with things untold or unspoken. Baba's adultery, Hassan's rape, and Amir's betrayal of Ali and Hassan are examples of things untold. One major unspoken thing in the boys' household is the difference between Pashtuns and Hazaras. Amir does not even know why the Pashtuns demean the Hazaras until he secretly reads a history book. It is only twenty-six years later, when General Taheri refers to Sohrab as a "Hazara boy," that Amir breaks his silence about this issue and demands respect for Sohrab. Another major unspoken truth in the household is the lack of mothers. Sanaubar gets little attention until the end of the novel, when she reappears in Hassan's life and redeems herself by caring for Sohrab. Baba maintains such silence about Amir's mother, Sofia Akrami that he assumes Baba blames him for her death. He learns more about her from the beggar in Kabul than he ever did from his own father. The key secret keeper and revealer in the story is Rahim Khan, who protects secrets for Baba, Ali, Hassan, and Amir. Ultimately, he is the one who insists on Amir's redemption.

Summary and Analysis of Chapters 4-6

Summary

Chapter Four

Chapter four opens with the story of how Ali became a part of Baba's family. In 1933, the same year Baba was born, two intoxicated young drivers struck and killed a Hazara couple. Only their five-year-old son, Ali, survived. Baba's father was asked to decide the young men's punishment. After sending the young men to serve in the army, he took Ali into his household. Baba and Ali grew up as quasi-brothers, just like Amir and Hassan a generation later. But despite their closeness, Baba never considered Ali his friend just as Amir never considered Hassan his. According to Amir, their ethnic and religious differences kept them from being true friends or family. At the same time, all these years later, Amir says Hassan is "the face of Afghanistan" to him. The boys played and got into mischief together like any other two boys, except that Hassan made Amir's breakfast, cleaned his room, and did all his other household chores. While Amir went to school, Hassan stayed home to do housework with Ali. After school, Amir would read to Hassan, who loved books despite his illiteracy.

One day, Amir pretended to read to Hassan from a book but made up his own story to trick Hassan. When Amir finished, Hassan clapped and told him it was the best story he had ever read him. Amir was so happy that he kissed Hassan on the cheek, and that night he wrote his first short story. It was about a man who had a cup that turned his tears into pearls. The man grew greedy and tried to find ways to make himself cry as much as possible. It ended with him sitting on top of a mountain of pearls, holding his wife's slain body. Amir took the story to Baba, but he refused to read it. Rahim Khan read the story and gave Amir a piece of paper on which he had written "Bravo." The rest of his note explained that Amir had achieved irony in his story, which is something many writers never manage to master. He encouraged Amir to put his talent to use. In the letter, he called Amir his friend, and for a moment Amir wished that Rahim Khan was his father instead of Baba. He was so overcome with guilt that he vomited.

Amir rushed down to where Hassan was sleeping on a mattress with Ali and woke up his friend. After hearing the story, Hassan proclaimed that Amir would be world-famous someday. However, he also pointed out a plot hole in the story. He asked why the protagonist did not just smell an onion to make himself cry instead of killing his wife. Amir was speechless.

Chapter Five

Before Amir could respond to Hassan's criticism of his story, gunfire erupted outside. The boys huddled together with Ali until Baba came home. For the first time, Amir saw fear on his father's face. He was even glad for the violence for a moment, because Baba held him and Hassan close. The events of that night, July 17, 1973, were a precursor to the end of life as Afghanis knew it. What would follow was the Communist coup d'etat of 1978, followed by the Russian occupation beginning in December of 1979. On that July night, the king's brother, Daoud Khan, had seized Zahir Shah's kingdom while he was away. Afghanistan had gone overnight from a monarchy to a republic. Tired of listening to the radio news, Amir and Hassan went to climb their favorite tree. On the way, a young "sociopath" named Assef and his friends confronted them. He taunted Hassan for being a Hazara; Assef also had a habit of taunting Ali, whom he called *Babalu*. He praised Hitler and then said that he wanted to finish what Hitler started and rid Afghanistan of Hazaras. He called Amir and Baba "a disgrace to Afghanistan" for taking in Hazaras. Just as Assef threatened to punch Amir with his brass knuckles, Hassan pointed his slingshot at the bully and threatened to take out his eye. Assef and his friends retreated, but promised to come back for Amir and Hassan later.

On Hassan's birthday, Baba summoned him to the house as usual to collect his present. To Hassan, Amir, and Ali's shock, Baba had hired a plastic surgeon to correct Hassan's harelip. Amir was jealous that Baba was giving Hassan such special attention. The surgery went well and Hassan could finally smile an unbroken smile. Ironically, Amir explains, it was soon after that Hassan stopped smiling for good.

Chapter Six

Chapter six opens in winter. Amir loved the icy season because the school was shut down for its duration. But he loved winter even more because then he flew kites with Baba, the only activity that consistently brought them closer. The pinnacle of winter for every boy in Kabul was the yearly kite-fighting tournament. Every year, Amir and Hassan saved their allowances to buy materials to make their kites, but they were not very good craftsmen. When Baba realized this, he started taking them to Saifo's to buy their kites, always buying the boys equally good kites. In the tournament, contestants used their kites' glass strings to cut others' kite strings until only one triumphant kite remained in the sky. Hassan was Amir's assistant. When kites fell out of the sky, especially the last kite to fall, those not flying their own kites would chase them and try to catch them-they were called "kite runners." Hassan was an exceptionally good kite runner. Once, Hassan convinced Amir to run the opposite way that a fallen kite was floating and sit under a tree with him to wait. While they sat, Amir taunted Hassan a little. Amir was unsettled to see Hassan's face change the way it sometimes did, as though there was an unfamiliar, sinister, hidden face behind his usual expression. After that uncomfortable moment, however, Hassan's face changed back to normal and the coveted kite came floating into his open arms.

In the winter of 1975, Amir watched Hassan run his last kite. That year, there was to be the biggest kite tournament the boys had ever seen. Boys from several neighborhoods would be competing in Amir and Hassan's neighborhood, Wazir Akhbar Khan. One evening, Baba suggested that Amir would win the tournament this year. After that, Amir became determined to win so that he could finally prove to Baba that he was a winner and a worthy son. The night before the tournament, Hassan and Amir huddled under blankets playing cards while Baba, Rahim Khan, and Assef's father met in the next room. Upon hearing that Afghanistan might get television under president Daoud Khan, Amir promised to buy Hassan a television set one day. Hassan responded that he would put it on the table in his and Ali's hut. Amir was dismayed than Hassan had accepted his fate of always living in the hut and being a servant. As though he read Amir's mind, Hassan told him, "I like where I live."

Analysis

Chapter Four brings attention to the theme of tragedy and violence that pervades the novel. We already know about Amir's violent birth, in which his mother hemorrhaged to death. Now we learn that tragedy was the reason Baba's father brought Ali into their family; he was orphaned by a terrible car accident. Hassan and Ali's physical problems were not caused by violence. Still, Hassan's harelip and Ali's stunted leg and lazy mouth make them targets for ridicule and violence. The fact that they bear physical signs of suffering while Baba and Amir do not reflects that they are people whose lives are defined by violence and hardship. The source of Amir's guilt is not so much the violence inflicted on Hassan, but his own exemption from violence. Indeed, it is only when Assef beats him almost to death that he feels "healed" of this guilt. Amir says, "...History isn't easy to overcome. Neither is religion. In the end, I was a Pasthun and he was a Hazara, I was Sunni and he was Shi'a, and nothing was ever going to change that. Nothing." In truth, it is not religion but suffering that separates the boys. True, Amir is a Shi'a all his life and Hassan is a Sunni. Yet when Amir has a split lip and suffering to match Hassan's, he can begin to reconcile their troubled history.

In Chapter Five, war and political turmoil enter the story. Even as a child, Assef is the bastion of this theme because he is a violent person who has no regard for others' emotions or suffering. He reveres Hitler and thinks that Hazaras do not deserve to live, facts that influence his decision as an adult to join the Taliban and joyfully slaughter Hazaras in Mazar-i-Sharif. From the beginning of the novel, Amir understands that things beyond his control have great influence over his life. When war enters the story, this fact becomes clearer than ever. Suddenly, no one is safe, no matter what privileges they have or what they believe; anyone can be killed by a stray landmine, bomb, or bullet. The riots in 1973 were a comparatively gentle precursor to the devastation that would follow under the Russian occupation and then the Taliban.

Chapters Five and Six introduce kite fighting and kite running, activities that bring Amir and Hassan closer together but eventually cause a permanent rift between them. In kite fighting, as in any activity, the difference between Amir and Hassan is obvious. Even though Baba makes a point of buying the boys equally nice kites, Hassan relegates himself to holding the string and running the kites for Amir. Just as he is Amir's household servant, he is his kite-fighting servant. His loyalty to Hassan extends so far that he puts himself in grave danger with Assef instead of running away. As we know, he ends up suffering rape because he is so intent on being a good servant and friend and retrieving the winning kite for Amir. At the same time, kite fighting is an activity that allows Hassan to show how special he is. We got a taste of Hassan's almost eerie perceptiveness when he criticized Amir's short story; though an illiterate boy, he was able to point out a major flaw in Amir's writing. Just as Hassan did not need to see the words on the page to know that Amir's story was flawed, he does not need to look at a kite or its shadow to know where it is going to land.

Kite fighting brings Amir closer not only to Hassan but to Baba. It is the only sport at which he is proficient, which matters greatly to strong, athletic Baba. Amir admits, "Baba and I lived in the same house, but in different spheres of existence. Kites were the one paper-thin slice of intersection between those spheres." Amir feels so neglected by Baba that his longing for Baba's love and respect lead him to betray Hassan not once, but twice. Amir's victory brings him closer to Baba than ever before, a fact that Hassan's rape would have overshadowed; because of this, Amir does not stand up for Hassan or tell anyone about the rape. Later on, when his guilt becomes unbearable, Amir prefers to drive Hassan and Ali out of the house rather than admit to what happened and risk losing Baba's affection. The kite fighting incident underscores the sense in the novel that every action has a consequence or a price. In exchange for his newfound closeness with Baba, Amir must give up his closeness with Hassan.

Kite fighting occurs only twice in the novel, yet the title is devoted to it and it becomes synonymous with the themes of betrayal and retribution. After twenty-six years, Amir still remembers Hassan as "The Kite Runner" because the activity represents both the happiness he and Hassan once felt together and the incident that parted them forever. Amir feels "healed" when Assef beats him nearly to death and he pays retribution for his sin when he adopts Sohrab, but things are still grim because Sohrab will not speak or interact with anyone. It is when Amir runs a kite for Sohrab that things truly come full circle. Amir saves Sohrab from physical harm, but only very reluctantly; Rahim Khan has to trick him into bringing Sohrab to America. Amir is selfish in his charity, not wanting to have another person's blood on his hands. Yet when he runs the kite for Sohrab, he shows true loyalty and selflessness because he is no longer trying to allay his guilt; he is trying to truly save Sohrab by restoring his faith in life.

Summary and Analysis of Chapters 7-9

Summary

Chapter Seven

The morning of the tournament, Hassan described his dream to Amir. In it, the two boys amazed the people of Kabul by swimming in a lake and proving it contained no monster. Then the boys were lauded as heroes and became the lake's owners. When Amir said he didn't want to fly a kite, Hassan told him, "no monster," and convinced him to proceed. Amir and Hassan were a great team and theirs was one of the last two kites left in the sky. Their hands were bloodied from holding the sharp string, but their hearts were filled with hope of winning the tournament. Amir focused hard and to his surprise, he cut the last, blue kite and won. The true victory for Amir was seeing Baba hollering with pride. Hassan took off to run the blue kite and Amir followed after bringing his kite home. A merchant told Amir that he had seen Hassan running by with the blue kite. He finally found Hassan facing Assef and his two friends, who were trying to steal the kite from him. Assef told Hassan that even Amir considered him worthless, but Hassan defended himself and Amir, saying that they were friends. Amir stood frozen in shock as the fight began.

The chapter is interrupted with Amir's memories, which appear in italics. The first is of Ali's words about his kinship with Hassan because they had the same nursemaid. The second is of Amir and Hassan visiting a fortune teller who gets a look of doom on his face while reading Hassan's fortune. Next is a dream, also in italics. Amir is lost in a snowstorm until he takes Hassan's outstretched hand in his. Suddenly the boys are in a bright, grassy field, looking up at colorful kites.

Amir transports us back to the moment when he hid in the alley, watching Assef and his friends seizing Hassan. He remembers the blue kite and Hassan's pants lying on the ground. Assef told both his friends to rape Hassan, but they refused. They consented to hold Hassan down while Assef raped him. Amir saw "the look of the lamb," the look of defeat, on Hassan's face.

The chapter is interrupted by another italicized memory. Baba, Ali, and their sons gathered in the yard to sacrifice a lamb for Eid-e-Qorban, in honor of the prophet Ibrahim's near sacrifice of his son. A mullah makes the meat halal and the tradition is to give one third to family, one third to friends, and one third to the poor. Baba's tradition is to give all the meat to the poor because he says, "The rich are fat enough already." Just before the mullah slaughtered the lamb, Amir saw its look of acceptance, as though it understood that its death was for "a higher purpose." The look would haunt him forever after.

We return to Hassan's rape. Amir turned away, weeping, still hearing Assef's grunts issuing from the alleyway. Instead of standing up for Hassan the way his friend had for him so many times, he fled. Amir tried to convince himself that he ran out of fear, but he knew that he felt Hassan to be his sacrificial lamb, the one to suffer for him so that he could live happily. In spite of himself, Amir thought, "He was just a Hazara, wasn't he?"

Some time later, Amir found Hassan walking down the streets, holding the blue kite. He pretended that he hadn't seen the rape, but he was terrified that Hassan would know or worse, would show him devotion despite knowing. Hassan said nothing about the rape even though he was bleeding through his pants. The boys returned home and proud Baba wrapped Amir in his arms. Amir was so overjoyed that he momentarily forgot that he had just betrayed Hassan.

Chapter Eight

After the rape, Hassan did not spend time with Amir although he still did his chores. A worried Ali asked Amir about Hassan's torn shirt and bloodied pants the night of the tournament, but Amir pretended not to know what happened. That night, he asked Baba if they could go to Jalalabad; ever since Amir won the tournament, Baba had not denied him anything. When Baba suggested they invite Hassan along, Amir told him that Hassan was sick. Amir looked forward to having Baba to himself, but Baba invited three vans' worth of relatives and friends along. As they drove along in the car, one friend's twin daughters recounted Amir's victory at the kite-fighting tournament. At this, Amir's carsickness overwhelmed him and he vomited. As they aired out the van on the roadside, Amir saw Hassan's bloodied pants in his head.

Finally, they reached Kaka Homayoun's house in Jalalabad. Even though Amir finally had the intimacy with Baba he had wanted all his life, his guilt made him feel emptier than ever. As Amir, Baba, and everyone else slept in the same room, Amir confessed to the darkness, "I watched Hassan get raped." No one heard him. He realized that he was the monster in Hassan's dream and had dragged Hassan to the bottom of the lake. That night, Amir's insomnia began.

A week later, Hassan asked Amir to climb the hill with him and read to him. When they reached their favorite spot, Amir changed his mind and the boys walked back down. After that incident, Amir's memories of the winter of 1975 are unclear. He could not wait for winter to end and school to begin, even though he had fun with Baba. He made sure to never be in the same room as Hassan, although his loyal friend kept trying to make things better between them. One day, after Amir refused to walk to the market with him, Hassan asked Amir what he had done wrong. Amir told Hassan that he should stop harassing him. After that, Hassan left him alone. One day as they were planting tulips, Amir asked Baba if he would get new servants. Baba was furious and threatened to strike Amir if he ever suggested it again. Ali and Hassan were their family, he said.

When school started, Amir was relieved to have homework to keep him busy. Then one day, he asked Hassan to climb the hill with him to hear a new story. Hassan joined him eagerly. After they picked pomegranates, Amir asked Hassan what he would do if he threw a pomegranate at him. When Hassan said nothing, he threw the fruit at him and demanded that Hassan throw one back. As Hassan refused to fight back, Amir threw countless pomegranates at him until he was stained in blood-red juice. Finally, Hassan smashed a pomegranate against his own forehead and asked, "Are you satisfied? Do you feel better?" before leaving.

That summer, Amir turned thirteen. Even though the coldness between him and Baba had returned, his father threw him a lavish birthday party with a guest list of four hundred people. Assef showed up with his parents and charmed Baba. He invited Amir to come play volleyball at his house and to bring along Hassan, but Amir refused. Then Assef offered Amir his gift, a book he picked out himself. After awkwardly excusing himself, he unwrapped the present alone; it was a biography of Hitler, which he threw into the bushes. Rahim Khan found him and told him a story. He had almost married a Hazara woman, but his family was outraged at the proposition and sent her and her family out of town. Then Rahim Khan told Amir that he could confide in him, but Amir could not bring himself to tell his friend what he had done. Rahim Khan gave him his present, a notebook for his stories. Then they hurried back to the party to watch the fireworks. In one flash of light, Amir saw Hassan serving drinks to Assef and Wali. He saw Assef playfully punch Hassan in the chest before, to his relief, the light faded.

Chapter Nine

The morning after his birthday party, Amir opened his presents joylessly. To him, each gift was tainted with Hassan's shed blood. He knew Baba never would have thrown him such an extravagant party if he had not won the tournament, and to him the victory was inseparable from Hassan's rape. Baba himself gave Amir a coveted Stingray bicycle and a fancy wristwatch, but they too felt like "blood money." The only gift Amir could stand to enjoy was the notebook from Rahim Khan. As he considered Rahim Khan's story about his Hazara fiancÃ©e, Amir decided that either he or Hassan had to leave their household in order for them to be happy.

When Amir took his new bike for a ride, Ali and Hassan were in the yard cleaning up the mess from the party. Ali stopped Amir to give him a present from himself and Hassan, a new copy of the *Shahnamah*, the book from which he had so often read to Hassan. When he got home, Amir buried the book at the bottom of his pile of presents so it would not torment him with guilt. Then he began scheming how to get rid of Hassan. Before he went to bed, he asked Baba if he had seen his new wristwatch.

The next morning, Amir hid his wristwatch and a bundle of cash under Hassan's bed. Then he told Baba that Hassan had stolen from him. Baba called a meeting with Ali and Hassan in his office. When they arrived, their eyes were red from crying. Hassan lied and said that he had stolen Amir's wristwatch and money. Amir felt a pang of guilt because he understood that Hassan was sacrificing himself for him as usual. He also understood that Hassan knew everything about the night he was raped, that Amir stood by and did nothing to help him. To his shock, Baba forgave Hassan, but Ali and Hassan had already resolved to leave. From Ali's cold glance, Amir understood that Hassan had told him about the rape and about Amir's nonaction. Despite Baba's begging, Ali and Hassan left. When they were gone, Amir saw Baba cry for the first time. As though echoing Baba's grief, the skies opened up and it stormed during the dry season in Kabul.

Analysis

In Chapter Seven, we finally witness Hassan's rape, to which Amir has been alluding since Chapter One. Hassan's comparison to the lamb underscores the theme of sacrifice. Hassan is a very brave person, but in the fight with Assef and his friends he does not go down fighting. Rather, he accepts his fate-he gets "the look of the lamb" in his eyes-because his loyalty to Amir makes him willing to suffer even the terribly violent act of rape. Amir, in contrast, is not willing to sacrifice anything for Hassan. Amir is so selfish that he ends up forcing Hassan and Ali out of the house rather than risking the loss of Baba's pride in him. *The Kite Runner* can be considered Amir's journey of learning how to be unselfish and make sacrifices for other people. Even when Rahim Khan makes it his dying wish for Amir to bring Sohrab to Peshawar, Amir tries to make excuses. Ultimately, he goes seeking Sohrab not so much to save the boy, but to save himself from his lifelong guilt. As we have said, it is in the act of running the kite for Sohrab that Amir is finally unselfish. He transforms from the kite fighter, seeking personal glory and attention, to the kite runner, unselfishly bringing joy to someone else.

In Chapter Seven, Hosseini uses italicized memories to represent Amir's emotional dissociation during the rape. In the alley, he is overcome by fear and he sees images. Some of them are of his and Hassan's solidarity: their being nursed by the same woman, their holding hands, their looking up at kites together. Some of them are manifestations of doom: the sacrifice of the lamb and the visit to the fortuneteller. By breaking up the chapter with harried memories, Hosseini makes it clear that Amir was in a state of panic and internal conflict. Still, he makes a conscious decision to abandon Hassan, whom he feels on some level to be his "sacrificial lamb" and "just a Hazara." In light of this, we can see the interruption of italicized memories as a representation not only of Amir's confusion and panic, but the moment when he became a true coward. We could dismiss the act of running away because Amir was a frightened child, but after the rape, his fear of being discovered and his capacity for betrayal only intensifies. As Amir says in Chapter One, that moment in the alleyway defined the rest of his life and, twenty-six years later, sent him on a quest for redemption.

Amir's guilt begins to consume him immediately after the rape. He becomes an insomniac. He cannot bear to be around Hassan, who reminds him of his guilt by merely existing. Instead of making him right his wrong, Amir's guilt leads him into a cycle of wrongdoing. First, he lies to Ali and says that nothing happened to Hassan.

Next, Amir begins to ignore Hassan, effectively torturing him with silence and compounding his injury. The only thing that sickens Amir as much as his guilt is the fact that Hassan will not do anything to stand up for himself. The incident with the pomegranates embodies Hassan's insistence on 'taking the high road' when it comes to violence and anger. Instead of pelting Amir with pomegranates, he smashes one into his own forehead, as though he is truly incapable of hurting someone else. Later, we find out that even after Amir drove him out of Baba's house, Hassan considered Amir "the best friend he ever had" and passed onto Sohrab his belief in nonviolence. Hassan's name means "handsome," which is ironic because people make fun of Hassan's appearance; in another sense, it is perfectly fitting because Hassan's inner beauty and purity of spirit is what makes him such a respectable and lovable character. When Amir throws the pomegranates at Hassan, he is begging for Hassan to absolve him by hurting him. Instead, his torture continues; he sees juice running down Hassan's shirt like blood, reminding him that Hassan's blood is on his hands. In the end it is Assef who "heals" Amir by hurting him.

Chapters Seven, Eight and Nine contain clues that Hassan and Amir are brothers and bring into question the idea of family. When Amir watches Hassan get raped, he thinks of Ali's stories about the Hazara woman who nursed them both, and about the fact that they have a special connection because they "nursed from the same breast." When Amir suggests to Baba that they get new servants, his father threatens to hit him for the very first time and says that Hassan and Ali are their family. Baba is quick to forgive Hassan even when he admits to stealing from Amir, begs them to stay, and weeps when they leave anyway. From one perspective, we cannot blame Amir for feeling disconnected from Hassan and Ali; after all, he was raised to know them as servants-cherished ones, but servants nonetheless. Amir's name even means "prince," making it seem as though he should hold such a view. From another perspective, Hassan and Ali are human beings and it is cruel of Amir to treat them as inferior. Amir's actions toward his relatives, even though he does not know they are, call into question the importance of family ties.

In the story, there is a significant difference between being *like* family and being family. Even though Hassan is *like* a brother to Amir-"the person whose first spoken word had been [his] name," he still betrays him. When Amir discovers that Hassan was indeed his brother, he feels he must make things right. For him, the blood connection gives new validation to their relationship because he realizes that they really were equals. Suddenly, all Amir's feelings of entitlement-to his privileges and to Baba's affection-change because he understands that Hassan deserved those things, too. Family ties also bring Amir a new sense of entitlement to Sohrab. When Amir visits the orphanage in Karteh-Seh, his being the boy's half-uncle gives him legitimacy. Family ties also prove an obstacle; in order to prove that Sohrab is an orphan, Amir needs proof that the boy has no other family, that his parents are dead. It is ultimately family, Soraya's cousin Sharif, who makes it possible for Sohrab to come to America.

Nearly everything Amir does wrong, he does in order to win or keep Baba's attention and affection. His actions come out of his deep-seated belief that Baba blames him for his mother's death. He does not find out until many years later that Baba was blaming himself all along, for shaming Ali and not being able to treat Hassan like a true son. According to Rahim Khan, Baba was hard on Amir because he was trying to raise him to be like himself but more righteous. The irony is that in trying to redeem his own honor, Baba raised a child who felt neglected and who acted out in fear. When Amir wins the kite tournament, he bridges his and Baba's worlds through a sport. His true wish, however, is for Baba to acknowledge his special talent for writing. He says, "Maybe Baba would even read one of my stories. I'd write him a hundred if I thought he'd read one. Maybe he'd call me Amir jan like Rahim Khan did. And maybe, just maybe, I would finally be pardoned for killing my mother." From this statement, we also know that Rahim Khan is in many ways more of a father to Amir than Baba. Rahim Khan is the one who encourages Amir to write and buys him the special notebook that he keeps for so long. He is also the one who holds Amir accountable for his sins and for Baba's. Not surprisingly, Rahim's first name means "compassionate"; he is the person who understands people and protects them both by keeping their secrets and by making them atone.

Summary and Analysis of Chapters 10-12

Summary

Chapter Ten

When Chapter Ten opens Amir and Baba are being smuggled out of Soviet- or *Shorawi*-occupied Kabul along with other Afghanis. Their goal was to reach the safer territory of Pakistan. Amir still has carsickness at age eighteen, which embarrasses Baba. The truck stops so that Amir can vomit on the roadside. Amir thinks of how secretly they had to leave Kabul, telling no one, not even their servant. The *rafiqs*, or Communist comrades, had taught everyone in Kabul how to spy on their neighbors and even their family.

The truck was supposed to have no trouble crossing through the Russian-Afghani checkpoints because of the driver, Karim's connections. At a checkpoint, the Afghani soldiers would have let the truck pass without issue, but one Russian soldier demanded a half hour with one of the refugees, a married woman. To Amir's dismay, Baba defended the woman, telling the Russian soldier that he had no shame and that he would "take a thousand bullets before [he] let this indecency take place." Amir felt ashamed that while Baba would give his life to save someone, he did nothing to save Hassan. The Russian soldier aimed the barrel of his gun at Baba's chest, but the shot that rang out did not kill him. It came from the gun of a more senior Russian soldier, who apologized for the first one, explaining that he was on drugs. The truck passed the checkpoint safely and in the darkness, the woman's husband kissed Baba's hand.

When the refugees finally reached Karim's brother's house in Jalalabad, he told them that his brother, Toor's, truck had broken the week before and could not take them to Peshawar, Pakistan. Baba smashed Karim against the wall and began to strangle him, furious that Karim had lied to them in order to take their money. Only the married woman's pleas stopped Baba from killing Karim. It turned out that there were many other refugees in the house, who had been waiting there for two weeks. Amir, Baba, and the others went into the basement to wait with them. Waiting there with them in the damp, rat-infested basement were Amir's schoolmate, Kamal, and his father. Kamal had a sunken look in his eyes, and his father explained to Baba that his wife had been shot and Kamal had been raped.

Because it turned out that Toor's truck was irreparable, the refugees departed in the tank of fuel truck. Before they left, Baba kissed the Afghani dirt and put some in his snuff box to keep next to his heart. Later, Amir awoke in the fuel tank feeling as though he was suffocating. He comforted himself with the memory of a spring afternoon he spent kite-fighting with Hassan. When they finally got out in Pakistan, they were thankful to be alive. Yet Kamal had suffocated on the fumes and died. In a rage, Kamal's father put the barrel of Karim's gun in his mouh and shot himself.

Chapter Eleven

Chapter Eleven opens in the 1980s in Fremont, California, a year and a half after
Amir and Baba arrived in America. Amir explains that Baba loved "the *idea* of
America" so much that it gave him an ulcer. He believed that the only worthwhile
countries were America, Israel and Britain, even though his support of Israel drew
accusations from other Afghanis of his being anti-Islam. He was the only Republican
among their blue-collar neighbors and even hung a framed picture of Ronald Reagan
in their apartment. One day, Baba got into a fight with Mr. and Mrs. Nguyen, the
owners of the small grocery store across the street. Mr. Nguyen had asked for Baba's
ID when he wanted to pay with a check and Baba was so insulted that he damaged
their property. It was clear to Amir that Baba missed their old life in Kabul and was
having trouble adjusting to America. Whereas in Kabul he had been wealthy and
influential, in Fremont he worked long hours at a gas station and missed almost
everything about home. He saw life in America as a gift he had given to Amir and
something he would have to suffer. For Amir, America was an escape from his
memories of Hassan.

Amir graduated from high school at the age of twenty, when Baba was fifty. After
the ceremony, Baba took Amir to a bar, where he bought drinks for other patrons and
became the life of his own impromptu party. When they drove home, Amir was
shocked to find that Baba had bought him a Ford Torino to drive himself to junior
college. When they went inside, Baba said he wished Hassan was there. Amir's
throat closed up with guilt. Amir also had to grapple with Baba's disappointment that
he wanted to be a creative writer instead of a doctor or lawyer. Amir found release
from his guilt by driving his Ford for hours at a time and sitting by the ocean. He was
grateful to be starting anew in America.

The next summer, when Amir turned 21, Baba bought an old Volkswagen bus. On
Saturdays, he and Amir drove to yard sales in neighboring towns and then sold their
wares at the San Jose flea market. The flea market was a cultural epicenter for
Afghan families, who dominated the Used Goods section. One one such day, Baba
introduced Amir to General Taheri, an old acquaintance of his from Kabul. The
"casually arrogant" Taheri did not impress Amir, but his daughter, Soraya, entranced
him. Baba told Amir that Soraya had had a relationship with a man that did not work
out well and had not been courted since. This did not matter to Amir, who already
thought of her as his "Swap Meet Princess."

Chapter Twelve

Amir's desire for Soraya tormented him. At the flea market, he made excuses to walk
by the Taheris' stand just to get a glimpse of her, but he could not muster the courage
to talk to her. Finally one Sunday, he asked Soraya what she was reading. This was
not a casual question in the Afghani community, because two single young people
chatting invited gossip. Soraya knew that Amir was a writer and said she would like
to read one of his stories. Just then, Soraya's mother, Kamila (or Khanum Taheri),

showed up and greeted Amir warmly. She was a nice woman with one peculiarity; one side of her mouth drooped. Khanum Taheri sent Amir off with fruit and asked him to visit again. Amir understood that Khanum Taheri, and perhaps the General, saw Amir as a suitor for Soraya.

Every week, Amir visited the Taheris' booth when the General was away. He chatted with Khanum Taheri and Soraya. He found out that like him, Soraya was attending junior college. She wanted to be a teacher. She told Amir how, as a child in Kabul, she taught her illiterate housekeeper, Ziba, how to read. Amir was ashamed, remembering how he had lorded his literary over the oblivious Hassan. Just as Amir handed her a story to read, General Taheri arrived at the booth and Soraya was forced to hand him the story out of propriety. He dropped it into the garbage can. Then General Taheri took Amir aside and scolded him for having such an open conversation with Soraya in the marketplace.

Later that week, Baba caught a terrible cold but did not wan to go to the doctor. Amir convinced him to see a doctor when he saw that Baba was coughing up blood. The doctor told Amir that there was a suspicious spot on Baba's lung that he needed to have checked out. That night, Amir prayed for the first time in a very long time. They finally got to see a specialist, Dr. Schneider, but Baba lost his temper when he found out the doctor was Russian-American. They found a new Iranian doctor, Dr. Amani, who discovered that Baba had terminal cancer. Baba refused to prolong his life with chemotherapy and made Amir promise not to tell anyone about his disease. After the diagnosis, Amir and Baba still went to the flea market on Sundays. As the weeks progressed, Baba lost weight and got sicker until one day, he fell on the ground and started having seizures.

At the doctor's office, the doctor showed Amir Baba's CAT scans. The cancer had spread to Baba's brain and he would have to take medications and receive radiation. Once news spread that Baba was dying, many local Afghans came to pay their respects, including the Taheris. Baba refused radiation, so Amir took him home to die. Then Amir asked him to ask General Taheri to go *khastegari,* to ask for Soraya's hand in marriage. Baba called and made arrangements to visit the Taheris the next morning. Amir helped Baba dress and drove him to the Taheris' house, then went home to wait. Finally, Baba called and said that the general had accepted and then put Soraya on the phone. She was delighted but said she wanted to tell him a secret. When the Taheris lived in Virginia, she ran off with an Afghan man. When her father found her and dragged her home, she found out that her mother had suffered a stroke that paralyzed the right side of her face. Amir was slightly upset to find out that Soraya was not a virgin because he was. At the same time, he knew that he of all people could not hold someone accountable for her past mistakes, so he told Soraya that nothing could change his desire to marry her. Envy tempered Amir's joy because Soraya was now free of her shameful secret whereas his still plagued him.

Analysis

Beginning in Chapter Ten, Amir is yanked out of his predictable, privileged life and thrust into one of uncertainty and hardship. Knowing Amir and Baba as we have come to, it is difficult to think of them as refugees, leaving everything they have and know behind in order to save their own lives. Because we know Afghan history, we know that Baba might have lost everything anyway, had he stayed to see the Taliban rule and the United States bomb the land. In newspapers and on the news in recent years, we have seen pictures of refugees and of starving, injured Afghan refugees. It seems as though Hosseini chose to focus on the a wealthy family's experience to show us what a good, prosperous life was like in Afghanistan. He makes the point that it was not always a wrecked country, even though it has been for as long as many Americans have known about it.

Amir is eighteen when he and Baba flee to Pakistan, meaning that it has been years since Ali and Hassan left. Indeed, he mentions that they have had several different servants in the intervening years. Still, Amir is not at all free from his guilt. Hosseini even introduces Kamal as a foil for Hassan. Like Hassan, Kamal has been raped and no longer smiles. His death and his father's subsequent suicide suggest one horrifying possibility of what might have happened to Hassan and Ali without Baba's protection. It is also a warning of what could easily happen to Baba and Amir. So much has changed since Amir was a boy, yet Baba still has the same unflappable courage. When Baba stands up for the married woman, it is the last time we ever see him in his element, in a position of power and defending those who are helpless. Once Baba and Amir come to America, Baba can never be the same because he is no longer in a position to help others.

The theme of sacrifice returns in Chapter Eleven, where we see how much Baba has given up in order to ensure Amir a better future. Once a party-giver and benefactor, Baba is now a gas-station worker in a country where he does not even speak the language fluently. He has gone from living in a large, luxurious house to living in a small apartment. Once the person everyone else could depend on, Baba now depends on Amir to help him navigate American life. The incident with the Nguyens makes it clear how out of place Baba is in California. As Amir explains, in Afghanistan the only 'credit card' they had was a branch into which a vendor carved a notch for each item bought. When Baba loses his temper after Mr. Nguyen asks him for ID, he is not being irrational; he comes from a place where such a request would have signified extreme distrust. While living in America is hard for Baba, it is a dream come true for Amir. Fremont, California is free of all the places and things that remind him of Hassan, his "harelipped ghost." As he says, "America was different. America was a river, roaring along, unmindful of the past. I could wade into this river, let my sins drown to the bottom, let the waters carry me someplace far. Someplace with no ghosts, no memories, and no sins. Amir can set his mind on new goals and let the optimistic American spirit carry him as far away from Kabul emotionally as he is physically.

To Baba's disappointment, Amir is the same person in Fremont as he was in Kabul. He still wants to be a writer. However, their relationship grows closer out of necessity; having lost almost everything familiar, they cling to one another. When Amir graduates from high school and Baba wishes Hassan was there, Amir feels a now-seldom pang of guilt. He does not realize that Baba is feeling worse guilt, because Hassan is his son and deserves the same opportunities as Amir. As Amir will surmise later, Baba may feel closer to Amir in America because Amir is more like Hassan there, struggling, no longer protected by privilege. As much as Amir wants to be swept up in the "river" of America, he is still rooted to Afghan tradition there because of the large community of refugees. From the moment he lays eyes on Soraya, he commits to preserving his roots because she comes from a traditional family.

Amir and Soraya's traditional courtship creates a little Afghan oasis in the confusion of America, which Baba and the Taheris greatly appreciate. As immigrants, even "former ambassadors, out-of-work surgeons, and university professors" are reduced to selling used goods at the flea market. Baba is a gas station worker and General Taheri a welfare recipient, in the matter of their children's courtship they feel like important Afghan men again. They are able to live in this reverie until Baba's diagnosis. From that point on, Amir must watch his father go from a strong, almost legendary figure to a shrunken, weak ghost of his former self. As though to add insult to injury, the cancer spreads to Baba's brain, the source of his intelligence and his trademark unapologetic opinions. In getting married, Amir restores Baba's dignity by showing him how much he is needed. Amir needs Baba to go *khastegari,* to give word at *lafz,* and to sit with him at the *awroussi.* Even in his pain and weakness, Baba feels good again because he has an important role to play. Seeing Amir and Soraya's traditional courtship and wedding also reassures Baba that Amir will not forget where he is from after Baba dies.

At the end of Chapter Twelve, Amir's guilt reappears. As he listens to Soraya's story, he pities her because he knows she is subject to a sexual double standard. But once Soraya is betrothed to Amir, her parents can stop worrying that no one will ever want to marry her. Amir envies Soraya for freeing herself from her guilt and for being a braver and better person than him. Her sin may be smaller than his, but she has the strength to admit to it at the risk of losing him. Amir himself does not reveal his sin until fifteen years later, when he calls her from Islamabad. Only when he has no choice can Amir admit out loud to what he has done because for him, "America [is] a place to bury [his] memories."

Summary and Analysis of Chapters 13-16

Summary

Chapter Thirteen

Chapter Thirteen begins at the Taheris' house with "*lafz,* the ceremony of "giving word." Even though Baba is very ill, he proclaims it "the happiest day of [his] life." Baba made a speech and General Taheri welcomed Amir into his family. Then Soraya joined the celebration and kissed Baba's hands. Traditionally, *lafz* is followed by an engagement party called *Shirini-kori* and an engagement period, but everyone agreed that they should skip it because Baba was so close to death. Baba spent almost all the money he had left on the traditional Afghan wedding ceremony, called *awroussi.* According to the ceremony, Amir and Soraya were left alone together under a veil to gaze at each other's reflections in a mirror. There, Amir told her he loved her for the first time. Amir could not help wondering whether Hassan had gotten married and what his wife was like. The party continued until the early morning, after which Amir and Soraya made love for the first time.

Soraya moved in with Amir and Baba after the wedding so that Amir could spend his father's last days with him. Soraya cared for Baba as though he were her own father, bathing him, reading to him, cooking for him, and giving him anything else he needed. One day, Amir came home to find Soraya hiding Rahim Khan's notebook under Baba's mattress. Baba admitted that he had coaxed Soraya to read him Amir's stories. Amir left the room to cry tears of joy, since he knew Baba disliked seeing him cry. A month after the wedding, Soraya's family came over to Baba's for dinner. Amir could see how happy Baba was to see him happily married. At the end of the night, Soraya and Amir helped Baba into bed. He refused his morphine, saying, "There is no pain tonight." He died in his sleep.

Baba's funeral took place at a nearby mosque. The men's and women's sections of the mosque were separate, so Amir sat next to General Taheri while Soraya and her mother were in another room. Amir acknowledged that Baba was his obstinate self until the end; he even died "on his own terms." Countless people whom Amir had never seen shook his hand and told him how Baba had helped them in one way or another. As he listened to their remarks, Amir realized that he no longer had Baba to define him or guide him; he felt terribly alone. After the burial, Amir and Soraya walked through the cemetery together and Amir cried at last.

After Baba's death, Amir got to know the Taheris much more closely. General Taheri was a complicated man. He did not work and collected welfare because he considered this more dignified than taking on a blue collar job as Baba had. He suffered from terrible headaches lasting days, and spent the rest of his time waiting for the liberation of Afghanistan. He felt sure that he would be called back to serve in the government at any time, so he always wore his grey suit and watch in preparation to leave. Khanum Taheri was a talented singer, but the general forbid her to sing. Instead, she focused her energies on homemaking. Now that Soraya was married, Khanum Taheri focused much of her attention on Amir. She adored him especially because he listened to her long list of imagined ailments; ever since her stroke, she became convinced that every small disturbance in her body was a serious ailment. Amir knew that Khanum Taheri was grateful to him not only for this, but for relieving her of her greatest fear-of Soraya becoming a spinster.

One night, Soraya told Amir the story of how the general forced her to end her affair. He came to her lover's house and told him he would kill him and himself if Soraya did not come home. Soraya told her father she wished he was dead, but she came home with him. At home, he made her cut off all her hair. Ever after, Soraya heard derogatory whispers everywhere she went. After Soraya told Amir the story, he asked her never to mention it again. He understood too well the torment of guilt and betrayal, but he also pitied Soraya for being a woman in Afghan society; even in America, she was subject to a double standard regarding sexual behavior.

Amir and Soraya moved into their own apartment. The Taheris helped them furnish it, and the general gave Amir a typewriter. They both enrolled at San Jose University, where Amir worked toward a degree in English and Soraya, in teaching. In 1988, Amir finished his first novel, "a father-son story set in Kabul." Soon after, he got a lierary agent and became a published writer. Amir's feelings of success were tempered with his guilt; he felt himself to be undeserving. That same year, international politics were particularly fraught. The Soviets withdrew from Afghanistan, but a new conflict erupted between the *Mujahedin* and the remaining communist government. The Berlin wall was destroyed and the Tiananmen Square riots occurred. In their safe American abode, Amir and Soraya began trying to conceive a child.

After months of trying to conceive, Amir and Soraya consulted fertility doctors. Neither of them had any detectable fertility problems, but they were still unable to have a child. When they told Soraya's parents, General Taheri and Khanum Taheri were disappointed. The general urged them not to adopt, most of all because Afghan society depends on the line of succession, which the act of adoption obliterates. Amir thought privately that his and Soraya's infertility was punishment for his betraying Hassan so many years before. Soon after they discovered they could not have a family, Amir and Soraya bought a house. Despite their newfound material comforts, the absence of a child tormented them both.

Chapter Fourteen

Chapter Fourteen opens in June of 2001, when Amir received a call from Rahim Khan. He told Amir he was very sick and asked him to come visit him in Pakistan. Amir considered what Rahim Khan had said before hanging up, "Come. There is a way to be good again." Suddenly, he understood that Rahim Khan knew, and had always known, what he did to Hassan. Amir was comfortable leaving Soraya with her parents; her relationship with them had improved in the years since the wedding. The General no longer insisted that Soraya change her career path away from teaching; sometimes he sat in on the classes Soraya taught and even took notes. That night, Amir dreamt of Hassan as he had seen him right before the rape, shouting, "For you, a thousand times over!" A week later, he left for Peshawar, Pakistan.

Chapter Fifteen

As Amir rode through the streets of Peshawar in a cab, he remembered being there in 1981 as a refugee. The city was bustling with vendors, families, and children. Rahim Khan was staying in the Afghan section. Amir had last seen him the night before he and Baba fled Kabul, and has barely spoken with him since. When Rahim Khan answered the door, Amir saw how emaciated his illness had made him. Still, Rahim Khan's face brightened in Amir's presence and at the news of his marriage fifteen years earlier. He did not remember the notebook he gave Amir.

Rahim Khan described how the Taliban was terrorizing Afghanistan, though they had been received initially as heroes. Once, at a soccer game, a man next to him cheered too loudly. A Talib pistol whipped Rahim Khan, thinking he had made the noise. People in Kabul were afraid to leave their houses because of frequent shootings and bombings. Even Baba's orphanage had been destroyed, with many children inside it. Then Rahim Khan told Amir that he did not have long to live. He laughed at Amir's offer to take him to America, saying he accepted his fate. Then he revealed to Amir that for all the years he lived in Baba's house after 1981, Hassan lived there with him. He told Amir that he needed a favor of him, but first wanted to tell him about Hassan.

Chapter Sixteen

Chapter Sixteen is in Rahim Khan's voice; he is telling Amir the story of what happened to Hassan. He went searching for Hassan in 1986 because he was dreadfully lonely, so many of his relatives and friends having been killed or fled since 1981. He was managing to take care of the house and himself despite his age and arthritis, but when the news of Baba's death reached him, he felt the weight of it all was too much. He drove to Hazarajat, where Ali and Hassan had been living, and was directed to a village outside Bamiyan. He found Hassan, now in his early twenties, and his pregnant wife, Farzana, living in a small hut. Hassan was overcome with joy when he saw Rahim Khan. He told him that Ali had been killed by a land mine two years before. He asked many questions about Amir. Initially, Hassan and Farzana refused to move to Baba's house, but then Rahim told him of Baba's death. Hassan cried all through the night and in the morning he agreed to move in with Rahim Khan.

Despite Rahim Khan's protestations, Hassan and Farzana stayed in the servants' hut and did all the chores. Hassan also wore black for forty days in mourning for Baba. In the fall, their daughter was stillborn; they buried her and Hassan placed a flower on her grave every day. Then in 1990, Farzana became pregnant again and Hassan's mother, Sanaubar, came to find him. She collapsed at the gate of the house; when they carried her inside and removed her *burqa*, they discovered that the former beauty was malnourished, had no teeth, and had grotesque scars all over her face from being cut. Hassan ran out of the house and was gone for hours, but when he returned he accepted Sanaubar as his mother. She became healthy and a part of the family; she even delivered Farzana and Hassan's son. Hassan named him Sohrab, after the hero in his favorite story from the book Amir used to read him. Sohrab became inseparable from Sanaubar, whom he called *Sasa*. Four years later, Sanaubar died peacefully. Hassan tried to give Sohrab a good childhood despite the constant fighting and danger in Kabul. He even took him kite running in the winter. When the Taliban took over, most people celebrated, but Hassan knew Hazaras' lives were in peril. He was right; in 1998 the Taliban "massacred the Hazaras in Mazar-i-Sharif."

Analysis

Just as the courtship had made Baba feel important again, so did the wedding. Knowing he is dying, he spends almost all his money on the ceremony, rings, and traditional clothing. Yet even had Baba not been dying, he would have wanted the wedding to be extravagant; it is his last chance to throw a grand party and feel as he once did in Kabul. The wedding also brings Amir back to Kabul momentarily, when he wonders about Hassan. Though Baba is reduced to having Amir and Soraya care for him in the last days of his life, his death restores his dignity once again. At the funeral, the Afghan community recognizes Baba for the man he was in Afghanistan. It is a small consolation for Amir, who feels more alone than ever before. Now he is alone not only with his sin and guilt but with all his decisions and his future. He says, "Listening to them, I realized how much of who I was, what I was had been defined by Baba and the marks he had left on people's lies. My whole life, I had been "Baba's son." Now he was gone. Baba couldn't show me the way anymore; I'd have to find it on my own." Despite the fact that he and Baba were estranged for much of his life, it is only now that Amir realizes he must form his own identity, independent of Baba.

When Amir and Soraya try to have a child, the idea of retribution makes a grand re-entrance. Because no medical explanation exists for their infertility, Amir decides that it is a result of his betraying Hassan. The silence that grows between him and Soraya over their inability to conceive is filled with Amir's feeling of responsibility for it. When General Taheri discourages the couple from adopting, he makes the case that adoption disconnects the family line and threatens the family's security. He says, "Blood is a powerful thing ... And when you adopt, you don't know whose blood you're bringing into your house." What neither he nor Amir knows is that adopting will allow Amir to continue his family line and also redeem himself from having wronged family so many years before. When Rahim Khan calls from Pakistan, he sets Amir's redemption into motion. Like Amir, Rahim Khan believes that life has certain inevitabilities; as he puts it, "There is such a thing as God's will." Just as certainly as he knows he is going to die, he knows that Amir must be the one to save Sohrab.

In Chapter Fourteen, we finally revisit the phrase that Amir mentions in Chapter One: "there is a way to be good again." Now we understand its magnitude; for the first time, Amir discovers that someone, Rahim Khan, knows his secret and has kept it for all these years. What he does not realize is that Rahim Khan does not want to be saved; he wants to save Amir. From the moment Amir sees Rahim Khan, it becomes clear to us how irrevocably Afghanistan has changed. Amir says, "A thing made of skin and bones pretending to be Rahim Khan opened the door." Their meeting is out of place-in Peshawar instead of Kabul-and so is Rahim Khan's appearance. The old man does not even remember the notebook that has meant so much to Amir for the last fifteen years. Yet once they begin to talk, it becomes clear how close they still are and how much influence Rahim Khan has over Amir.

Because guilt has plagued Amir all these years, it is surprising that he does not seize the opportunity to redeem himself. Rather, he is evasive and keeps forcing Rahim Khan to raise the stakes for him. When Rahim Khan plays his best card and tells Amir that Hassan was his brother, and that he needs to redeem Baba as well as himself, Amir storms out like an angry child. Suddenly, he understands what it is like to be betrayed. Later we find out that Rahim Khan knows Amir better than the latter ever thought. He realized that Amir would resist bringing Sohrab to America, so he made up the story about the Caldwells. Amir does save Sohrab by bringing to America, but only after he is effectively tricked into doing so. This is why it is the act of running the kite at the end that truly redeems Amir; unlike all the other heroic things he does, it is of his own volition and out of the spirit of true selflessness and loyalty.

Through Rahim Khan's words in Chapter Sixteen, we learn that Hassan remained a loyal and humble person until death. Even though he never found out Baba was his father, he still mourned for him the way a son does. He insisted on living in the servant's hut and keeping house for Rahim Khan, presumably out of respect to Baba and also to Ali, who never asked for anything more. Hassan was as forgiving as an adult as he was as a child. When Sanaubar returned decades after abandoning him, he merely took time to collect himself and then returned to welcome her with open arms. And as Sohrab tells Amir later, Hassan even forgave Amir and considered him "the best friend he ever had." In the end, Hassan died defending Baba's house and honor.

Rahim Khan and Hassan bring the war stories from Afghanistan alive for us before we see them through Amir's eyes. Both men describe public beatings at the slightest provocation. Sanaubar is forced to wear a *burqa,* as we know, on pain of death. The men's firsthand knowledge of these things highlights their difference from Amir. Whereas they are Afghans to the very end, Amir seems to have lost his connection to his identity. As he stated before, he was 'carried away' by America's promise of a fresh beginning without memories of Hassan or what he did to him. Amir had been exempt from violence the moment he boarded the plane to California, but Rahim Khan and Hassan remained surrounded by danger. They had come to know a new, though terrible, Afghanistan, while Amir had tried as hard as he could to forget all about it. Even before Farid points out the fact point-blank, we can see that Amir has become a foreigner in his own homeland. At the same time, he is very much the person he was. It is true that in America, Amir experienced suffering and hardship, from having to learn English to not having money to seeing Baba degraded to watching him get sick and die. But Amir returns to Afghanistan in many ways just as he left it: he is a person of privilege, a person who is afraid to stand up for others, and a person who does not want to take responsibility for his actions. Back on Afghan soil, he must finally learn to be what Baba wanted him to be, and what Wahid calls him later on - "a true Afghan."

Summary and Analysis of Chapters 17-19

Summary

Chapter Seventeen

After Rahim Khan finished telling the story about him and Hassan, he handed Amir a letter and a photograph. The photograph was of Hassan and Sohrab. In the letter, Hassan described the violence and injustice in Afghanistan. One day, Farzana spoke slightly loudly in the market and a Talib beat her so hard that she fell down and was bruised for days. Despite the terror, Hassan said, Sohrab was a healthy and smart boy; Hassan had made sure he was literate and knew how to shoot a slingshot as well as his father. Hassan ended his letter by expressing his wish to see Amir in Afghanistan again. Rahim Khan explained that the letter was written six months before. A month after he had arrived in Peshawar, he received news of Hassan's death from a friend. After he left Kabul, word spread that a Hazara family was living alone in Baba's house. One day, the Taliban came to the house and demanded that they leave. When Hassan protested, they took him out to the street, forced him to kneel, and shot him in the back of his head. Farzana ran out screaming and they shot her dead as well. The news devastated Amir, who could only whisper, "No. No. No."

Rahim Khan explained that the Taliban now occupied Baba's house and they were not held accountable for Hassan and Farzana's murders. Then he told Amir that he real reason he made Amir come to Peshawar was to bring Sohrab there. An American couple named Thomas and Betty Caldwell ran a goodwill organization there and would take care of him. When Amir protested and suggested Rahim Khan hire someone to find Sohrab, Rahim Khan was insulted. He told Amir, "I think we both know why it has to be you, don't we?" Then he asked Amir if he had become what Baba feared so many years before, a person who "can't stand up to anything." He said it was his dying wish for Amir personally to bring Sohrab to Peshawar. When Amir continued to refuse, Rahim Khan revealed a monumental secret. Amir and Hassan were half-brothers. Ali was infertile, as evidenced by the fact that his first wife bore him no children, but bore her second husband three daughters. It was Baba who had gotten Sanaubar pregnant, making Hassan his son. Rahim Khan explained that no one but himself, Baba, Ali, and Sanaubar had known about the matter in order to preserve their honor. Hassan never found out. Amir was furious at all of them for keeping the secret. He screamed at Rahim Khan and left the apartment.

Chapter Eighteen

After storming out of Rahim Khan's apartment, Amir had tea at a local cafΓ©. He felt like a foreigner in his own life. Now that he knew Hassan was his half-brother, it seemed absurd that he had not realized it before. Baba had always treated Hassan like a son not just because he cared for him, but because Hassan was really his son.

Amir wondered how Baba could have broken his own cardinal rule about not lying, how he could have lived with himself after shaming Ali.

Suddenly, Baba did not seem like such a shining example of righteousness. Amir now understood that Rahim Khan had called him to Peshawar to pay not only for his betrayal of Hassan, but for Baba's betrayal of Ali. Amir wondered if he was to blame for Hassan and Ali's deaths because he was the one who drove them out of the house and split up the family. Finally, at thirty-eight years old, Amir was ready to take responsibility for his actions. He returned to Rahim Khan's apartment to find him praying and told him he would bring Sohrab to Peshawar.

Chapter Nineteen

A driver named Farid was driving Amir from Peshawar to Kabul. He was a Tajik man of twenty-nine, who looked much older because of all he had experienced, fighting against the Soviet forces. Farid had two wives and seven children, two of whom had been killed by a landmine. Farid himself was missing toes and fingers from his years of combat. Farid was suspicious of Amir because he saw him as a defector; whereas Farid had stayed and fought for his homeland, Amir had fled to the privileges of America. He had abandoned his *watan,* his homeland.

Amir felt awkward in his traditional Afghan clothing and long fake beard, both necessary for him to blend in to Taliban-controlled Kabul. He told Farid, "I feel like a tourist in my own country," who replied, "You still think of this as your country?" Amir said he did because he had grown up there, but Farid explained to Amir that he had never been a true Afghani because he grew up with so many privileges. Amir did not try to argue with Farid. At last, they arrived in Jalalabad, where they would spend the night with Farid's brother, Wahid.

Unlike Farid, Wahid received Amir warmly. When he found out Amir was a writer, he suggested Amir use his writing to "tell the rest of the world what the Taliban are doing to [Afghanistan.]" Amir explained that he was "not quite that kind of writer." When Wahid asked Amir why he had returned to Afghanistan, Farid interrupted. He ranted about how people returned their only to be greedy and milk money out of their old properties. Wahid scolded Farid for his rudeness. Then Amir explained why he was really in Afghanistan. At this, Wahid called him, "An honorable man ... A true Afghan." Farid was ashamed at his own presumptuousness. Later he apologized to Amir, who told him, "You were more right than you know."

One of Wahid's wives brought dinner to Amir and Farid, saying the family had eaten earlier. As he ate, Amir noticed that Wahid's three boys were staring at his watch. After asking for Wahid's permission, he gave it to them. To his surprise, it did not impress them very much. Amir slept restlessly, dreaming about Hassan's death. He imagined that he himself was the Talib executing Hassan. When Amir woke up, he paced outside and pondered the fact that Afghanistan really was his homeland. His loyalty to the country surprised him, since he had built a new and full life in

America. From inside, Amir heard one of Wahid's wives scolding him for not leaving any food for the children; Amir realized that the boys had been staring not at his watch, but at his food. Before he and Farid left the next morning, Amir tucked a wad of money under a mattress for them to find.

Analysis

Chapter Seventeen brings the subject of literacy into clearer focus. The ability to read and write divided Amir and Hassan when they were boys. Being literate when Hassan was not gave Amir a feeling of superiority over him, causing him to abuse his privilege by playing tricks and being secretly cruel. Hassan's illiteracy does not mask his intelligence; for example, he points out the major plot hole in Amir's story. But as an adult, Hassan realizes that not being literate puts him at a disadvantage and makes him depend on others. For this reason, he makes sure that Sohrab can read and write even though it breaks his family tradition. Even though Hassan feels entitled to very little all his life, he does feel that he has a right to knowledge; as usual, what matters to Hassan is intangible and enduring. The letter is of course significant because of its content, but it is perhaps more noteworthy because of the simple fact that it is written. Hassan is communicating with Amir on an equal level, something he could never have done when they were boys. Hosseini gives a nod here to the power of the written word, which endures and has an effect that transcends even death-after all, Hassan is long dead by the time Amir reads his correspondence. This also gives legitimacy to Amir because, coward though he may be, he is a writer, an ambassador of the written word.

The topics of secrets and family ties converge and come to a climax in Chapter Seventeen, when Rahim Khan finally reveals to Amir that Hassan was his half-brother. Amir is furious because suddenly the way he treated Hassan and Ali seems all the more wrong. The concept of "brother" is much stronger to him than the concept of "servant-best-friend" whereas Hassan had treated him like a brother no matter what. As Amir says, "Hassan had loved me once, loved me in a way that no one ever had or ever would again." Amir's reaction to the news reveals how important family ties are anywhere, but in Afghanistan particularly. As General Taheri says in Chapter Thirteen, "People [in America] marry for love, family name and ancestry never even come into the equation. But we are Afghans." Among Afghans, one's family line determines much about how one's life will proceed, from whether one will be literate to whom one will marry. For instance, the reason the Taheris give Soraya to Amir so easily is because of Baba's good standing and ancestry. Hassan's not knowing his identity meant he missed many of the things to which he was entitled. Amir now feels as though his entire life has been "a cycle of lies, betrayals, and secrets," and not just his own. He finally understands that Baba was as much of a betrayer, liar, and secret-keeper as he is. He also understands that this makes the importance of his redemption twofold, saying, "Rahim Khan had summoned be here to atone not just for my sins but for Baba's too."

Amir's interactions with Farid and Wahid call into question the idea of homeland and national identity. Once he reached America, Amir clung to Afghan customs but insisted on forgetting his memories of Kabul. He welcomed America not for its idealism, as Baba had, but for the simple fact that it was not Kabul. To him, everything in Afghanistan was tainted with memories of Hassan, his "harelipped ghost." Amir's youth when he arrives plays a large role in his feelings about homeland and nationality. Because he is still growing up when he arrives, he is not as mired in Afghan traditions and attitudes as his father's generation. Over the course of fifteen years Amir has come to consider America his homeland, whereas General Taheri is still awaiting the moment when he will be called back to his beloved *watan*. Amir's opinion of Hassan has changed now that he knows they were brothers, but his connection to America is stronger than his feeling of obligation to anyone in Afghanistan. As he tells Rahim Khan, "*I can't go to Kabul ... I have a wife in America, a home, a career, and a family.*" When he finally consents to find Sohrab, Amir acknowledges his lack of loyalty to his fatherland. He admits, "I knew I had to leave as soon as possible. I was afraid I'd change my mind. I was afraid I'd deliberate, ruminate, agonize, rationalize, and talk myself into not going. I was afraid the appeal of my life in America would draw me back, that I would wade back into that great, big river and let myself forget."

Amir's disconnect from Afghanistan becomes even clearer when he is driving with Farid. Firstly, Amir is in disguise; in addition to his fake beard, he is wearing traditional Afghan clothing for maybe the first time in his life. Amir struggles with his separation from Afghanistan, because he still feels some entitlement to it; he says, "My mother had died on this soil. And on this soil, I had fought for my father's love." Farid quickly dispels any illusions of Afghan nationality that that Amir has when he says, "You've *always* been a tourist here, you just didn't know it." He points out that because he grew up with so many privileges, he never experienced the life of a typical Afghan. Farid sneers, "You probably lived in a big two- or three-story house with a nice backyard that your gardener filled with flowers and fruit trees. All gated, of course. Your father drove an American car. You had servants, probably Hazaras." Amir has to admit, albeit privately, that all of this is true. He grew up in one of the nicest houses in Kabul. Baba had driven a Mustang and proudly so. He did have a gated backyard, and it was Hassan and Ali who did their chores and tended the garden. It is only when Amir truly begins to reclaim his and Baba's honor that he also reclaims some of his Afghan identity. Wahid proclaims him, "an honorable man ... A true Afghan" only when he discovers that Amir is going to Kabul to honor his family ties.

Summary and Analysis of Chapters 20-22

Summary

Chapter Twenty

The devastation in Kabul took Amir's breath away. The buildings and streets had turned into rubble, and fatherless children begged on every street corner. When a red truck full of Talibs drove by, Amir was mesmerized by them for a minute. Farid warned him never to stand at the Talibs again, because they welcomed any chance to start a conflict. An old beggar overheard them, asked for change, and started a conversation; while chatting, he quoted a line from a poem Amir recognized. It turned out that the man was a professor who used to teach at the university alongside Amir's mother. It was now Amir who was begging the old man-for any details about his mother. He gave Amir just a few small details about her, which amounted to more than he had ever learned from Baba. Amir was deeply grateful. The old man directed him and Farid to the orphanage in Karteh-Seh.

A skinny man answered the door at the orphanage. He pretended not to know who Sohrab was until Amir begged, "I'm his half uncle." Once he trusted the men enough to let them in, he told them Sohrab was fantastic with his slingshot, from which he was inseparable. In the man's makeshift office, he explained that they had no heat or hot water and very little food or supplies. The Taliban refused to pay for renovations or improvements. The man did not seem to want to talk about Sohrab. When Amir insisted, he revealed that a Talib official had taken Sohrab a month earlier. This official came every few months and paid to take a child with him; the man had no choice but to consent, or he knew he and all his children would be shot. This news so enraged Farid that he tackled the man and tried to strangle him to death until Amir intervened. The man told Amir that he could find the Talib official at Ghazi stadium, where the national team played soccer.

Chapter Twenty-One

After Amir visited the orphanage in Karteh-Seh, the horrifying truth about Afghanistan fell upon him more and more rapidly. As he and Farid drove away, he saw a forgotten corpse hanging in front of a restaurant. He saw a man selling his artificial leg, no doubt to buy food for his children. When they reached the Wazir Akhbar Khan district where Amir grew up, he was relieved to see that it had weathered somewhat better than the other neighborhoods.

The chapter is interrupted by Amir's memory of finding a turtle in the backyard with Hassan. They painted its shell red and marched it around as though they were discoverers of a wondrous new species. Even though they were children, they felt as though they were world-renowned explorers.

Amir walked up the driveway to Baba's house and saw that it had fallen into disrepair. He longed for it to be as it once was. Despite Farid's protestations, he insisted on staying for as long as possible. Amir climbed the hill with the pomegranate tree as he had with Hassan so many times. Although the tree was now decrepit, he could still make out the carving from their childhood: "Amir and Hassan. The Sultans of Kabul." After he sat for a while in contemplation, he and Farid drove off and checked into a nearby hotel.

The hotel was just as run-down as the rest of Kabul and there was even a bloodstain on the wall near the bed. Before going to bed, Farid told him stories about fighting the Soviets. In return, Amir told Farid about American conveniences, such as being able to receive over five hundred television channels; Farid explained that Kabul had not even had electricity for days. Finally, the men bonded over jokes about the bumbling cleric, "Mullah Nasruddin." Before he fell asleep, Amir thought that perhaps Kabul was as "hopeless" as people said.

The next day, the men attended a soccer match at Ghazi Stadium. It was nothing like Amir remembered, the lush green playing field now turned to dry dirt with two deep holes behind the goalpost. Talibs walked up and down the aisles, whipping anyone who made too much noise. During halftime, Amir discovered the horrifying reason for the two deep holes in the ground; they were to be the graves of two accused adulterers, who would be stoned in front of the thousands of attendees. A cleric announced to the crowd that the "will of Allah and the word of the Prophet Muhammad" said death by stoning was a just punishment for adulterers. As he listened to this distortion of Islam, Amir e what Baba had said years before: "God help us all if Afghanistan ever falls into their hands."

The Talib official they had been waiting for appeared on the field. He personally stoned both of the accused to death, after which other Talibs buried them. Afterwards, Farid told a Talib that they wanted to arrange a meeting with the Talib official; it was very easy for them to get an appointment for the same day.

Chapter Twenty-Two

Farid and Amir parked in front of a large house in Wazir Akhbar Khan where the meeting would take place. Farid waited in the car while a terrified Amir went into the house. After being frisked by armed Talibs, he was ushered into an empty room. The Talib official entered the room and sat down opposite Amir, who noticed he had blood on his sleeve from the executions. He ordered one of his men to rip off Amir's false beard, then described with relish his role in the mass execution of the Hazaras. He derided Amir for leaving Afghanistan, saying he should have him shot for treason. Then he ordered Sohrab to come into the room. Sohrab's resemblance to Hassan shocked Amir, who saw that the boy wore bells around his ankles and makeup on his face. The Talib officer put on music, banned to everyone but the Taliban, and made him dance. Then he said to Amir, "Whatever happened to the old *Babalu*, anyway?" Horror filled Amir as he realized that the Talib official was Assef.

When Amir offered to pay for Sohrab, Assef explained that he did not need money; his wealthy parents lived on an Australian beachfront. Besides, he joined the Taliban not for money but because he felt it was his divine task. When he was in prison in the 1980s, there was a guard who beat one prisoner each night in order to terrorize the others. One night, when Assef had a terrible kidney stone, the guard decided to beat him. He was wailing in pain as the guard beat him until one kick to his side dislodged the kidney stone and made it pass so that he laughed through the rest of his beating. Assef believed it to be "a message from God." Years later, he found the same man injured on the battlefield and shot him in the genitals. Ever since, he had been "on a mission" to get rid of those he considered unworthy of living in Afghanistan.

Assef said Amir could have Sohrab, but he would have to kill Assef in order to leave the house. He told his guards to wait outside the room and not enter no matter what they heard. If Amir killed him, he would be able to go free. Then Assef told Sohrab to stay as a "lesson."

The chapter is interrupted briefly by Amir's memory of the doctor who helped nurse him back to health.

Amir describes the fight with Assef. Assef had used brass knuckles, his favorite weapon from childhood, to beat Amir and knock out his teeth. He remembers his ribs, a bone in his face, and his nose breaking. He remembers that at one point, he began to laugh uncontrollably; even though Amir's body was broken, his spirit finally felt healed. It was Sohrab who saved him in the end. Amir was lying on the ground with Assef on top of him, preparing for another blow, when Sohrab begged him to stop. He was aiming his slingshot at Assef's eye, just as his father had done half a century before. Assef tried to jump on Sohrab, who shot him and in doing so, gouged out his eyeball. As Assef rolled on the floor in pain, Sohrab helped Amir to the car. Farid drove away as fast as he could as Amir lost consciousness.

Analysis

Chapters Twenty through Twenty-Two showcase the devastation that reigns in Kabul under the Taliban. The theme of violence has been central to the novel all along in the context of Hassan's rape. However, in Taliban-controlled Kabul, Amir's personal nightmare erupts into a public reality. We already know that a single rape has influenced Amir's life immeasurably. When Amir and Baba were fleeing to Pakistan, they found out about a second rape, Kamal's. Now, we discover that under the Taliban, even government officials are raping children. The government's appetite for violence is insatiable; they not only jump on any existing chance to enact violence, but provoke people so they can beat them. As Farid explains, merely staring at a Talib is reason enough for him to injure someone. Both Hassan and Rahim Khan have described beatings by the Taliban merely for talking too loud. The Taliban have created a culture not only of violence but of humiliation.

Baba, General Taheri, and many other Aghan immigrants to America suffer humiliation because they are in an unfamiliar environment. Their job status is taken away from them because they are unfamiliar with American ways and the English language. He describes how "former ambassadors, out-of-work surgeons, and university professors" who had obviously worked hard to gain their status and wealth in Afghanistan reduced to selling at the flea market. As Baba's incident with the Nguyens shows, even small differences in custom can cause humiliation for an immigrant. Yet once Amir returns to Kabul, we see how much better the difficult lives of American immigrants are compared to those who stayed. Baba may have to sell other people's junk for money, but he is far luckier than the amputee in Kabul who is trying to sell his artificial leg. Above all, those who emigrated to America are alive, whereas most of the men in Kabul are dead, as evidenced by the countless fatherless children begging on street corners there. Once Amir sees how devastated Afghanistan has become, he understands what Farid said about him being a foreigner in his own homeland. It is as unfamiliar to him as "an old, forgotten friend [whom] life hadn't been good to ... Homeless and destitute."

In incorporating the stonings at Ghazi Stadium into his story, Hosseini brings to life something about which most non-Afghans have only heard. The event is all the more significant because we experience it through Amir's eyes-American eyes-eyes that are unaccustomed to this type of unchecked violence and injustice. Beyond their sheer violence, the deaths of the accused adulterers in Ghazi Stadium embody what is happening to the Afghan people under the Taliban. The victims are accused of being adulterers, but from what we know about the Taliban from Rahim Khan, Hassan, and Farid's accounts, they may just have looked at a Talib the wrong way. They are killed in public, supposedly to make an example for others; in truth, their public murders are meant to intimidate the masses and bring them under even closer control. Not just the two victims in Ghazi Stadium, but the Afghan people as a whole, are being dragged into a pit of hopelessness from which there is no escape, degraded, and killed cruelly and unjustly.

From the moment Amir makes a commitment to return to Afghanistan, things in the story begin to come full circle at an accelerated pace. In the moment when he hides money under Wahid's mattress, he is atoning for doing so fifteen years earlier. This time, instead of plotting to ruin one child's life, he is trying to make sure that three other children do not starve. Amir acknowledges the circularity of his journey when he ponders, "Once, over those mountains, I had made a choice. And now, a quarter of a century later, that choice had landed me right back on this soil." Once Amir finds out that the Talib official is Assef, the story's sense of circularity crosses over into the near impossible or even slightly magical. Amir himself cannot believe it. As he remembers, "The moment felt surreal-not, not surreal, *absurd*-it had knocked the breath out of me, brought the world around me to a standstill ...What was the old saying about the bad penny? My past was like that, always turning up."

Just like Amir's and Hassan's, Assef's childhood tendencies were a good predictor of how he would turn out as an adult. Amir seemed harsh when he called Assef a "sociopath" early in the story, but now we understand that he was not exaggerating. Assef has become like his idol, Adolf Hitler. He takes joy in massacring innocent people in the name of his own supremacy. Just as Assef raped Hassan so many years before, he is now raping and humiliating Hassan's son. The fight between Amir and Assef is surreal not just because Amir does not remember everything clearly, but because it is an echo of his confrontation with Assef when they were children. Years before, Hassan saved him with his slingshot and now, Sohrab saves him with his. Even the way Sohrab defeats Assef is eerily similar to the way Hassan threatened him-Hassan had aimed the slingshot at Assef's eye once before, and now Sohrab finishes what his father began.

When Amir feels his blood running down his face and his bones breaking, he feels gleeful. Throughout the story, Amir has done everything in his power to avoid violence. As a child, he let Hassan do his fighting for him and refused to stand up for himself, much less someone else. Despite Assef's taunting and promises of violence, Amir stands up for Sohrab and in doing so, for Hassan as well. When Assef rains violence down on Amir, it is as though every blame and injury that Hassan took for him is being returned to him all at once. When Amir demanded that Hassan throw a pomegranate at him, he had refused. Now, Assef is the one who gives Amir not only "what [he] deserve[s]" but what he longs for. Finally, he is being punished for what he did to Hassan. Even though Amir is aware that he could die, he feels "healed" of his decades-long affliction.

Summary and Analysis of Chapters 23-25

Summary

Chapter Twenty-Three

Amir is lying in his hospital bed, floating in and out of consciousness. He does not know where he is or how long ago he was brought in; all he can think of is that he wants to thank a child for something. In his fleeting moments of clarity, he sees a caretaker named Aisha, a doctor, and Farid-although he cannot remember names. Amir has a vision of Baba fighting a bear in Baluchistan, a story that is supposedly true. At the end of the vision, he sees that he is Baba.

When Amir finally regains full consciousness, the doctor, Dr. Faruqi, explains his injuries. He has had several surgeries in the two days since Farid brought him in; his jaw is wired together, his spleen ruptured and had to be removed, he suffered several broken ribs and a punctured lung, his upper lip was split open, and his eye socket bone broken. Dr. Faruqi said Amir was lucky to have survived such trauma. As Amir tried to take in the magnitude of what happened, one ironic fact stayed with him; he now had a harelip scar just like Hassan had.

The next day, Farid and Sohrab came to visit. When Farid asked what happened in the room with "the Talib official," Amir replied, "Let's just say we both got what we deserved." Farid told him that Rahim Khan had left Peshawar, leaving behind a key and a letter for Amir. Amir asked Farid to leave Sohrab with him for a few hours. Even though Amir tried to reach out to Sohrab and thanked him for saving his life, Sohrab was shy and refused to make eye contact. The day dragged on, but it was punctuated by the entrance of a strange man. He surveyed the room, stared at Amir, and left. Most likely, he was a spy sent by Assef to threaten Amir's life.

After Sohrab left, Amir read Rahim Khan's letter. In it, he revealed that Hassan told him about the rape soon after it happened. He told Amir that he did betray his friend, but reminded him that he was only a boy at the time. He assured Amir that he had suffered from his guilt so much only because he was a good, caring person. Rahim Khan explained that it was hard for him to watch Amir vying for Baba's attention. Baba, he said, was hard on Amir only because of his own guilt. His betrayal of Ali and the fact that he could never claim Hassan as his son tortured him. Rahim Khan believed that all of Baba's charity was in atonement for his sin. Amir, he said, should learn from Baba's example and try to redeem himself as well. He said he had left money for Amir in a safety deposit box, which the key would open. He ended the letter by requesting that Amir not look for him. Amir cried reading the letter. He was ashamed that, unlike Baba, he had acted out because of his guilt rather than doing good.

The next morning, Amir looked at his face in a mirror. His monstrous appearance shocked him. Then Farid came to visit. He warned Amir that they had to leave Peshawar right away before Taliban sympathizers tried to finish him off. Amir sent him to find John and Betty Caldwell and spent the day playing cards with Sohrab. They did not talk much, but eventually Sohrab told Amir what Hassan said about him, that he was "the best friend he ever had." Still, every time Amir tried to touch Sohrab's arm, he pulled away.

The next day, Amir left the hospital against Dr. Faruq's advice. He planned to use the money from the safety deposit box to pay his bills, leave Sohrab with the Caldwells, and fly home. When Farid arrived with Sohrab, he explained that there were no Caldwells in Peshawar, nor had there ever been. Farid drove Amir and Sohrab to Islamabad

Chapter Twenty-Four

Islamabad was much more modern and cleaner than Peshawar, and the hotel they stayed in even had a television-a big change from Kabul. Before Farid left to rejoin his family, Amir paid him a little over two thousand dollars, leaving his friend speechless. Sohrab fell asleep and then Amir did the same. When Amir awoke, Sohrab was gone. The hotel manager, Fayyaz, decided to help Amir find him, saying, "I will drive you because I am a father like you." They found Sohrab sitting in front of the giant Shah Faisal Mosque. Amir sat on the grass with Sohrab, who told him about his memories of his parents. Amir gave him the photograph that Rahim Khan took.

Sohrab asked Amir if he would go to hell for taking out Assef's eye. Amir told him that Assef was a bad man who had hurt Hassan many years before. He assured Sohrab that Hassan would have been very proud of him. Sohrab was tormented by a feeling that he was dirty because Assef and his men had molested him. Amir told him that he was not dirty and after some coaxing, Sohrab let him hold him in his arms. He asked Sohrab if he would come to America with him, but Sohrab only sobbed.

The issue of America lay dormant until a week later, when Amir and Sohrab took a day trip to a hill. There, he revealed to Sohrab that he and Hassan were half-brothers. Sohrab asked if Baba had loved him and Hassan equally, and Amir replied, "he loved us equally but differently." Back at the hotel, Amir promised to show Sohrab the Golden Gate Bridge and drive him up the steep streets of San Francisco. He promised Sohrab that he would never have to live in an orphanage again.

At last, Amir called Soraya. After fifteen years of marriage, he finally told her about Hassan's rape. She told Amir to bring Sohrab home. The next day, Amir took Sohrab to the American Embassy to see an official named Raymond Andrews. Amir told him he wanted to take his half-nephew to America, omitting all the information about Assef. Raymond Andrews told him that his chances of getting a visa for

Sohrab were slim. He would have to prove that Sohrab was legally an orphan by providing death certificates for Hassan and Farzana; this would have been impossible even in pre-Taliban Kabul. Before leaving, Amir snapped at Raymond Andrews, "They ought to put someone in your chair who knows what it's like to want a child." As he and Sohrab left, the receptionist told Amir that Raymond Andrews's daughter had committed suicide.

It turned out that Soraya's cousin, Sharif, might be able to get Sohrab a visa because he worked for the INS. In the meantime, a lawyer named Omar Faisal came to consult with Amir at the hotel. He grew up in Berkeley but spoke perfect Farsi. Amir told him the unedited story of what happened with Assef. He repeated what Raymond Andrews had said about death certificates, but said there was some hope of adopting Sohrab if he was placed in an orphanage temporarily.

After Omar Faisal left, Amir told Sohrab that he might have to spend a little time in an orphanage. Terrified, Sohrab sobbed and begged Amir not to put him in an orphanage, but Amir could not bring himself to promise. He knew that an orphanage might be their best hope. Finally, Sohrab cried himself to sleep and Amir fell askeep as well. A call from Soraya awoke him; she gave the good news that Sharif would be able to get Sohrab a visa. Amir knocked on the bathroom door to tell Sohrab that all their fears were over, but he would not answer. Then Amir opened the door to the bathroom and began to scream; an ambulance took him and Sohrab to the hospital.

Chapter Twenty-Five

Amir is at the hospital, waiting for Sohrab. He finds a bedsheet and kneels on it to pray for the first time in over fifteen years. He mumbles the phrases of prayers he still remembers, his belief in God suddenly renewed. In his prayers, he begs God to let Sohrab live; he will do anything to ensure the boy's safety, saying, "My hands are stained with Hassan's blood; I pray God doesn't let them get stained with the blood of this boy too." He recounts what he saw when he opened the bathroom door; Sohrab lay dying in the bloody bathwater, having slit his wrists with Amir's razor. Finally, a doctor tells Amir that Sohrab will live. When he finally gets to visit Sohrab in the intensive care unit, Amir sees how hopeless he is. At Fayyaz's request, Amit stopped staying in his hotel. He barely said a word, even when Amir read him the story of his namesake from the *Shahnamah*. Finally, he told Amir, "I want my old life back" and that he wishes he was dead. Amir told him the good news from Soraya and asked Sohrab to forgive him for going back on his word. Sohrab just said he was tired and fell asleep.

Eventually, Amir did bring Sohrab home with him to San Francisco. We discover that Amir has been narrating the story in 2002, seven months after they arrived. Sohrab had not spoken a single word since then. He showed no interest in the books Soraya had bought him or any activity they suggested. They did not tell the Taheris the story of why exactly they were adopting Sohrab or how Amir had gotten injured. One day, General Taheri said, "People will ask. They will want to know why there is a Hazara boy living with our daughter. What do I tell them?" Amir, angered, told the general that Sohrab was the son of his illegitimate half-brother and told him never to call him a "Hazara boy" in front of him again.

The political landscape had changed in the interim since Amir and Sohrab arrived home. The Twin Towers had fallen in New York City and The United States had bombed Afghanistan, compounding the damage done by decades of fighting. Amir found it strange to hear non-Afghan Americans discussing the cities of his childhood. He and Soraya began to get involved on Afghanistan's behalf, trying to restore a hospital on the Pakistani border. Amir had kept his promise to pray after Sohrab had survived his suicide attempt.

Amir explains that four days earlier, a miracle happened. He and Soraya took Sohrab to an Afghan picnic in the park, along with Khanum Taheri. General Taheri was not there because he had finally gotten his wish; he had been offered a post in the Afghanistan ministry. By now, people had gotten used to Sohrab's silence and even Soraya could not bear trying to engage him anymore. Only Amir kept trying. Suddenly, Amir noticed kites flying over the park. He bought one and brought it to Sohrab. He told him that Hassan was the best kite runner he had ever known and asked Sohrab to fly the kite with him. Sohrab remained silent, but Amir knew what to do; he ran as fast as he could to launch the kite. As he stared up at it, he noticed that Sohrab had followed him and handed him the string. Sohrab soon gave it back to him. They stood in silence once more until they noticed a green kite closing in on theirs. When the kite came close enough, Amir performed Hassan's favorite kite-fighting trick, "the old lift-and-dive" as Sohrab watched, mesmerized. The green kite fell out of the air. When Amir looked down at Sohrab, he witnessed a half-smile steal over Sohrab's face. He asked, "Do you want me to run that kite for you?" Sohrab nodded, and Amir told him, "For you, a thousand times over." Amir ran among the children, after the kite.

Analysis

Amir's recovery is the second time in the novel that Hosseini uses broken images to convey a sense of detachment from reality. The first was when Amir witnessed Hassan's rape in the alleyway. The most important image from Amir's recovery time is his dream about Baba wrestling the bear, in which he is Baba. The story about Baba and the bear was a neighborhood legend, which Amir had later taken to represent any trouble Baba went through. When Baba died, Amir called his cancer "the Bear he could not defeat." The dream is full of symbolism on many levels. One one level, Amir is Baba and Assef is the bear. Amir describes how "Spittle and blood fly; claw and hand swipe." He even says, "They fall to the ground with a loud thud," which also describes the moment just before Sohrab saved Amir. Amir knows that by escaping, he has bested Assef just as Baba supposedly killed the bear. On another level, the dream is about Amir coming to terms with his guilt, which the bear represents. When he puts himself in grave danger on Sohrab's behalf, Amir is challenging his guilt-challenging the bear. It is important that the dream ends with

Amir beating the bear but not killing it. Just as he does not kill the bear in his dream, Amir has not yet defeated his guilt. Only when he runs the kite for Sohrab is he redeemed.

In Islamabad, Amir finds out that he is not the only one living in a cycle of guilt; like many victims of cruelty, Sohrab feels responsible for what has happened to him. Sohrab's fears make it clear that he took his fathers life lessons to heart. Like Hassan and Ali before him, Sohrab believes in God and does not believe that people should use violence to solve their problems. Sohrab does not feel safe with Amir, and rightfully so since he has been abused by so many adults. He believes himself to be "so dirty and full of isn." However, that is not the only reason Sohrab's fears are justified. Amir is still putting his own needs in front of Sohrab's because he is acting out of his guilt. When Sohrab disappears from the hotel, Amir says, "I imagined Sohrab lying in a ditch. Or in the trunk of some car, bound and gagged. I didn't want his blood on my hands. Not his too." Because Amir is not yet acting selflessly towards Sohrab, it is ironic when the hotel manager says, "I will drive you because I am a father like you."

Hosseini takes us into the mundane yet necessary world of bureaucracy to show how international policies often compound people's experiences of trauma. Raymond Andrews is a figurehead for the red tape that one finds throughout American, or any, immigration policies. Amir has spent weeks feeling like a privileged American in compassion to the Afghans. Now, he feels like an Afghan speaking to a privileged American who does not understand him. Amir's feeling of separation from Raymond Andrews is particularly clear when he describes the way Andrews "press[es] his hands palm to palm, as if he were kneeling before the Virgin Mary." He knows that Raymond Andrews is a "typical American," and he interprets his gesture as such-his gesture reminds Amir of Christianity instead of Islam.

Amir is shocked, as perhaps we are, to discover that even the sharpest image of hardship is not enough to cut through America's red tape. The fact that Sohrab has been raped, enslaved, and possibly seen his parents slaughtered still does not exempt him from procedure. Amir suddenly finds himself identifying with Afghanistan more strongly than he has in years. He has authority in his voice when he tells Raymond Andrews, "This is Afghanistan we're talking about. Most people there don't have *birth* certificates." The moment when Amir leaves the Embassy is doubly significant. In the first place, it serves to reconnect Amir to his American identity, from which he has felt estranged while talking to Raymond Andrews. When Amir finds out that Andrews lost his daughter in a violent way, he is reminded that violence exists everywhere in the world, even in privileged societies and situations. In the second place, the moment uses one of Hosseini's favorite techniques, foreshadowing.

Sohrab's suicide attempt breaks up the calm that falls over the story in Islamabad. Once Amir knows that he and Sohrab are in a safe place, he assumes that they are free from violence. Despite the massive injuries he has sustained, Amir still does not understand what it means to be wounded in one's soul, to be a true victim of war. He also is not yet the father that the hotel manager thought him to be because he has trouble understanding just how young and vulnerable Sohrab is. Amir has not yet learned that breaking a promise to a child makes that child feel unsafe. And with the terror that Sohrab has withstood, not feeling safe takes on a whole new meaning. Most children are afraid of pretend monsters, but Sohrab has faced real ones. The way in which Sohrab tries to kill himself speaks volumes about the guilt he himself feels. Not surprisingly, Amir's assurances that he is not "dirty" do little to comfort him. Not only does he die in the bathtub, but he drains the blood from his veins as though dying that way will clean him of his guilt and all his painful memories.

In several ways, Sohrab's suicide attempt teaches Amir how strong an influence fear has over people's lives. It is fear and panic that drive him to pray after fifteen years and convince him that God exists. Amir suddenly understands that people who are afraid need to believe in God in order to maintain their hope. He says, "There is a God, there always had been. I see Him here, in the eyes of the people in this corridor of desperation. This is the real house of God, this is where those who have lost God will find Him ... There is a God, there has to be." Believing in God makes Amir resemble Hassan more, because he is suddenly pious like his friend. However, as Amir acknowledges, his prayers flow from a selfish locus. He is bartering with God, promising to be a more devout Muslim in exchange for Sohrab's life. He is still acting out of his long-held guilt, praying, "My hands are stained with Hassan's blood; I pray God doesn't let them get stained with the blood of this boy too ... I pray my sins have not caught up with me the way I'd always feared they would." From these words, it is clear that even though Amir desperately wants Sohrab to live, the person he is most concerned with is still himself.

In the end, Rahim Khan is the one who knows the true path to redemption. He tells Amir in his letter, "I know that in the end, God will forgive. He will forgive your father, me, and you too. I hope you can do the same. Forgive your father if you can. Forgive me if you wish. But, most important, forgive yourself." Rahim Khan understands that Amir takes pleasure in torturing himself with his guilt. As long as he is directing his remorse inwards, he cannot truly help anyone else. Only when he forgives himself and stops feeling the pain of guilt can Amir direct his full focus on repaying his debt to Hassan and Baba's debt to Ali. As he puts it, true forgiveness involves "pain gathering its things, packing up, and slipping away unannounced in the middle of the night." Once Amir has stopped merely 'not wanting to have blood on his hands,' he can make use of those hands. He does just that when he teaches Sohrab about kite fighting.

When Amir and Sohrab fight the blue kite, the story finally comes full circle. The sport takes Amir back to the moment before everything changed, when Hassan had not been raped and they were just two boys having fun together. He says, "I was twelve again." Now that Amir has forgiven himself, kite fighting reminds him of pleasure instead of pain. His memories no longer being painful, he shares them with Sohrab: "Did I ever tell you your father was the best kite runner in Wazir Akbar Khan? Maybe all of Kabul? ... Watch, Sohrab. I'm going to show you one of your father's favorite tricks, the old lift-and-dive." In the ultimate moment of circularity, Amir runs the kite for Sohrab just as Hassan ran his last kite for him half a century before. Finally Amir understands what it is like to be as loyal and loving as Hassan, and can truthfully repeat Hassan's words, "For you, a thousand times over." The kite is a symbol of Amir's good, fatherly wishes for Sohrab. He wants to bring him joy, opportunity, a sense of security, and the will to live again, if only this were as easy as bringing him the kite. The last time Amir went to find a kite, he ended up turning his back on Hassan for good by running away from the scene of his rape. This is why the novel's last words, "I ran," are so meaningful. Even though Amir's story has made a circle metaphorically speaking, it has not ended where it began. Amir is running in a positive way, away from Sohrab physically but toward him emotionally. He is finally running with freedom in his heart instead of fear.

Suggested Essay Questions

1. Could the story of the novel exist without the class difference between Amir and Hassan? Make a case, using specific plot points and historical facts to ground your argument.

2. Examine the concept of circularity in the novel. What important cycles exist in the characters' lives and histories? How is circularity connected to redemption?

3. Explore the way in which courage is portrayed in the novel. What constitutes true bravery? What are the key moments when characters are brave and who is the bravest character, if any? Use specific examples from the text to support your argument.

4. Each character in the novel is shaped not only by his particular circumstances, but by the historical and political events that occur during his life. Consider Sohrab, the only character of his generation; how is he different from the other characters and how are these differences a function of what he has experienced?

5. Consider the idea of a homeland or "watan." How do you think the novel defines a homeland? Make sure to consider the opinions of Farid and Assef. Also, consider this question in terms of Amir and Sohrab, two characters who leave Afghanistan when they are still growing up.

6. Even though countless events occur in the novel, the title refers to kite fighting and kite running. What do these activities represent in the novel and why are they so important? To whom or what does the title, "The Kite Runner," refer?

7. Examine what it means to be American in the novel. How do different characters see America and is there one perspective that comes across most definitively? Some characters you may want to consider: Amir, Baba, General Taheri, Omar Faisal, Farid.

8. Think about the fathers in the novel. According to the novel, what does it mean to be a father? How can one measure one's success at fathering? Some characters to consider: Baba, Ali, Amir, Hassan, General Taheri, Farid, Wahid, Raymond Andrews.

9. "Like father, like son." "The apple doesn't fall far from the tree." "Monkey see, monkey do." Use one of these cliches as a starting point to consider the way characters in the story behave. Characters to consider: Amir, Hassan, Assef, Baba, Sohrab, Rahim Khan.

10. Make a list of instances in the novel where someone is forgiven. What constitutes true forgiveness? Why is forgiveness so important? You may want to consider moments between Hassan and Amir, Baba and Hassan, Hassan and Sanaubar, Amir and Sohrab, General Taheri and Soraya, and Amir and himself.

11. Think about acts of violence in the novel individually and as a whole. Why is violence so essential to the story? Could the story occur without so much violence? Using your answer from the previous question, explain what you

think Hosseini is using violence to say. You may want to consider: Hassan's rape, Sohrab's rape, the stonings at Ghazi Stadium, Assef and Amir's fight, Sohrab's suicide attempt, the story of Kamal and his father, Hassan and Farzana's murders, Sanaubar's appearance at the house, and the activity of kite fighting.

The History of Afghanistan during the Time of The Kite Runner

The Kite Runner deals with the country of Afghanistan from the 1970s to the year 2002. Like all places, Afghanistan has a long and complicated history, but it came to international attention only after the coup of 1973. In order to orient ourselves, let us look at Afghanistan's geography. The nation is located in Central Asia and is made up of thirty-four provinces. The country's capital is Kabul, which is also the capital of the northeast province of the same name. Afghanistan means "Land of Afghan," Afghan being a name the Pashtun majority used to describe themselves starting before the year 1000. It is bordered by Pakistan, Iran, Tajikistan, Turkmenistan, Uzbekistan, and for a short distance, China.

From 1933-1973, Afghanistan was a monarchy ruled by King Zahir Shah. On July 17, 1973, when the king was on vacation, Mohammad Daoud Khan seized power. Mohammad Daoud Khan was Zahir Shah's cousin and a former Prime Minister of Afghanistan. The military coup was nearly bloodless, but as we see through Amir's story, it was still a frightening time for the people of Kabul who heard rioting and shooting in the streets. For six years, Mohammad Daoud Khan was President and Prime Minister of Afghanistan. Then, on April 27, 1978, he was violently overthrown by the PDPA, People's Democratic Party of Afghanistan. Daoud was killed in the coup along with most of his family. Even though Afghanistan had long insisted on maintaining its independence from Russia, the PDPA was a Communist party and therefore held close ties to the Soviet Union.

The PDPA instituted many political and social reforms in Afghanistan, including abolishing religious and traditional customs. These reforms incensed groups of Afghans who believed in adherence to traditional and religious laws. These factions began to challenge the government so rigorously that in 1979, the Soviet Army entered Afghanistan, beginning an occupation that would last a decade. This is the historical point in *The Kite Runner* when Baba and Amir leave Afghanistan. Throughout the ten years of Soviet occupation, internal Muslim forces put up a resistance. Farid and his father are examples in *The Kite Runner* of these *mujahedins* or men engaged in war on the side of Islam. The United States was among the countries that supported the resistance, because of its own anti-Soviet policies. When the Soviet Troops finally withdrew in 1989, Afghanistan remained under PDPA for three more years. Then in 1992, in the wake of the collapse of the Soviet Union and therefore Soviet support for the government, the *mujahedin* finally won Afghanistan and converted it to an Islamic State.

In the years following Soviet withdrawal, there was a great deal of infighting among rival militias, making everyday life in Afghanistan unsafe. In *The Kite Runner,* Rahim Khan describes the fear in Kabul during this time. He remembers, "The infighting between the factions was fierce and no one knew if they would live to see the end of the day. Our ears became accustomed to the rumble of gunfire, our eyes familiar with the sight of men digging bodies out of piles of rubble. Kabul in those days ... Was as close as you could get to that proverbial hell on earth." Then in 1996, the Taliban took control of Kabul. After so many years of insecurity and violence, the people welcomed the takeover. Rahim Khan remembers, "... We all celebrated in 1996 when the Taliban rolled in and put an end to the daily fighting." The Taliban were a group of Pashtun supremacists who banded together and took almost complete control of the country. Despite their warm initial reception, they soon made life in Afghanistan dangerous again. Being Sunni fundamentalists supremacists, they systematically massacred Shiites including the Hazara people. They also enacted fundamentalist laws, most famously those banning music and dance, and those severely restricting women's rights. In *The Kite Runner,* we see how the Taliban used fear and violence to control the people of Afghanistan, for example at the frequent executions in Ghazi Stadium.

After the events of September 11, 2001, the United States invaded Afghanistan and overthrew the Taliban. The end of *The Kite Runner* occurs in 2002, when a provisional government was in place. It was not until 2004 that the current president of Afghanistan, Hamid Karzai, was elected. Today, there are countless Afghan refugees living in other parts of the world, just like Amir and his family. For those Afghans living in Afghanistan, life is still dangerous. In the South, conflict continues to rage on and the Taliban have managed to reemerge. According to Amnesty International's 2007 report, violence and human rights abuses are still a common reality in Afghanistan due to weak governance.

Author of ClassicNote and Sources

Tania Asnes, author of ClassicNote. Completed on August 23, 2007, copyright held by GradeSaver.

Updated and revised W.C. Miller September 29, 2007. Copyright held by GradeSaver.

Hosseini, Khaled. The Kite Runner. New York: Riverhead Books, 2003.

Magnus, Ralph H. Afghanistan : Mullah, Marx, and Mujahid. Boulder: Westview Press, 2000.

Matinuddin, Kamal. The Taliban Phenomenon : Afghanistan 1994-1997. Karachi, Pakistan: Oxford University Press, 1999.

Grossman, Lev. "The Kite Runner Author Returns Home." Time Magazine. 2007-08-17. <http://www.time.com/time/magazine/article/0,9171,1622583,00.html>.

Sadat, Mir Hekmatullah. "Afghan History: Kite Flying, Kite Running and Kite Banning." Afghan Magazine. 2007-08-18. <http://www.afghanmagazine.com/2004_06/articles/hsadat.shtml>.

Sethna, Razeshta. "Interview with Khaled Hosseini." Newsline. 2007-08-17. <http://www.newsline.com.pk/newsnov2003/newsbeat4nov.htm>.

Essay: Amir's Quest for Salvation in The Kite Runner

by Anonymous
May 04, 2008

"There is a way to be good again" (Hosseini 2). Rahim Khan's first words to Amir in Khaled Hosseini's The Kite Runner set in motion Amir's attempt to mend his scarred past. A mentally tormented man until Khan's call, he has repressed memories from his childhood for decades. His journey to Afghanistan to seek redemption forms a way for him to realize what is truly important in life. Although Amir's unintentional barbarity to Hassan is terrible, he is able to overcome his past sins and achieve personal salvation by confronting his actions and doing good.

Amir is an ordinary boy and though his behavior harms Hassan, he is not cruel or sadistic. Rather, his evil deeds take a more benign form, disguised as a need to please his father. For example, when he prepares to take part in the annual Kabul kite flying contest, he declares to himself that he will "run that last kite… and show it to Baba. Show him once and for all that his son was worthy" (Hosseini 56). Amir's motivation for entering the contest is not to gain recognition or fame among his peers. Instead, his goal is to win over his father, who has constantly reminded Amir that he is not worthy of affection. Only a demonstration of physical skill, he reasons, will ever make Baba like him. Likewise, when he observes Assef brutally raping Hassan, Amir declines to intervene, instead rationalizing to himself that Hassan was merely "the price I had to pay, the lamb I had to slay, to win Baba" (Hosseini 77). Amir refuses to stop Assef's violation of Hassan because he realizes that Hassan's fate is irrelevant to whether or not Baba will bestow praise upon his son. Baba will not find out about Amir's cowardly behavior, and he will still gain praise and recognition from Baba. In fact, Amir "resents sharing his father's affection with the loyal and talented Hassan," and actually views Hassan's rape as an opportunity to become closer to his father ("Khaled"). If Hassan, humiliated and shamed by the brutal act, cannot bear to face or speak with other people, Amir will eliminate a former competitor for his father's affections. Caught up in an emotionally charged moment, Amir's only thought is to gain praise from his dear Baba. In the process, he commits the largest crime of his young life.

However, Amir is not intentionally malicious toward Hassan, so he later feels guilty. After finally celebrating his kite contest victory in Jalalabad with his dear Baba, Amir realizes that he is a "monster" (Hosseini 86). Amir fully grasps the enormity of what he has done: he has committed almost unforgivable sin against Hassan stemming from a childish, selfish desire to gain Baba's graces. However, instead of cowering in shame and blaming others or cursing fate, he accepts sole responsibility for his actions. Amir reveals that he is an otherwise good person, as he possesses a conscience and a sense of guilt. In fact, as Amir notices, the real danger that has arisen from his actions is "the nature of my new curse: I was going to get away with it" (Hosseini 86). What pains him most is the realization that there is no going back. No one would find out what he did. Secretly, Amir wishes that someone would find out and rat him out for his true nature. He cannot bear to live with the secret of his shameful deed, yet cannot bring himself to face it. Although he knows that no one will expose him, he attempts to right the wrong that he has done.

Despite his good intentions, Amir's attempt to conceal his evil causes him to perpetrate even more offenses. When first talking to Hassan after the rape, Amir throws a pomegranate at him and wishes that Hassan would strike back in return and "give me the punishment I craved, so maybe I'd finally sleep at night" (Hosseini 92). Amir knows the magnitude of the offense he has committed, and foolishly thinks that if Hassan retaliates, the retaliation will somehow mitigate the severity of his action. Amir begins to harm others while trying to make up for what he has done. His twisted logic is taken to the extreme when he decides that the only way that he can fully solve the problem he has created is to remove Hassan from the household: "The better to hide his own secret sin, Amir betrays Hassan a second time, resulting in Hassan leaving the relative paradise and safety of Baba's home" (Morace).

Ironically, the very thing that Amir wanted so badly (winning the kite competition), the very thing that finally brought him the praise of his dear Baba, is now the thing that figuratively tears him apart. Hassan's mere presence is a constant reminder of Amir's shame and guilt, a dark shadow that lingers to haunt him. Hassan's unwavering loyalty despite Amir's terrible treachery is even worse. Hassan's naivety and devotedness emphasize his purity and natural goodness, a sharp contrast to the emotionally tortured Amir. Consequently, when committing his second betrayal, Amir is only able to think of himself. Never does he consider the effect of his actions on Hassan or Ali. Regrettably, in parallel to the thickening web of lies and deception, Amir's behavior grows worse. For instance, after Baba confronts Hassan about "stealing" Amir's watch, Amir almost blurts out the truth, "except that a part of me was glad. Glad that this would all be over with soon" (Hosseini 105). Amir's selfishness and shortsightedness have now become his primary traits, causing more havoc than he could have imagined. He is actually is able to paint his dreadful treachery of Hassan as a hardship on himself, a burden that he would be relieved to get rid of. Amir begins to stop feeling emotions about others, replacing feelings for them with his own distorted view of reality. He has changed from an ordinary boy to one that uses a misshapen view of others to inflict suffering upon them. When he finally fully recognizes the extent of his treachery and sins, Amir is shocked at the pain that he has caused others.

Accordingly, Amir relentlessly tries to escape his betrayal of his former friend, but cannot do so. However, in his desperate quest escape, he learns of the healing power of confronting the past. Soon, the Soviets invade Afghanistan and force Amir and his father to flee to America, a place Amir "embraced" because it contained "no ghosts, no memories, and no sins" (Hosseini 136). Amir supposes that by physically moving away from his past he can finally be at peace with it. He welcomes America because it is a place where he will not have to muster courage to face what he did to Hassan.

He is, as Stella Algoo-Baksh notes, "convinced that his soul can be at peace now that he has left his past behind. Yet . . . Amir soon discovers that such a release is not easily achieved" (143). Although he does not think about it, his past still lurks in the deep recesses of his mind, haunting him, mocking him for his cowardliness. Ironically though, it is America where Amir learns his first lesson about remembering the past. His wife, Soraya, had a shameful history of her own, but she came out immediately and told him about it, and for that, he "envied her. Her secret was out. Spoken. Dealt with" (Hosseini 165). Amir admires how Soraya sets herself free by revealing her past. She relishes knowing that people accepts her as she is, even with her flaws and mistakes of long ago. However, Amir refuses to acknowledge his past and constantly lives in fear that those he loves would reject him upon learning of what he has done. Despite his important realization, Amir is reluctant to confront his past as he is still afraid that others will criticize him for it.

Only when prodded by a close friend, Rahim Khan, does Amir finally find the strength to confront his past. At first, when Khan calls to ask Amir to return Afghanistan, Amir wishes that "Rahim Khan hadn't called me. I wished he had let me live on in my oblivion" (Hosseini 226). This statement is the last remaining bit of Amir's crumbling resistance to facing his past. Although Amir verbally expresses dismay at Khan's call, he has secretly hoped that this moment would come. He realizes that it is impossible to forget about one's past, and actually wanted someone to spur him to action and give him the courage to face his past misdeeds. The deciding factor is secrecy. Now that somebody already knows what he has done, Amir can tackle his history without fearing that his past actions will then be discovered. In essence, he is freed from the threat of new shame because his secret is already known. Later on, when he does fly back to Pakistan to meet Khan, Amir learns that Baba was the father of Hassan and is he shocked at his father's behavior. However, as Khan notes, the good that Baba did in his life "was all his way of redeeming himself. And that, I believe, is what true redemption is, Amir jan, when guilt leads to good" (Hosseini 302). Amir recognizes that Baba did not hide in disgrace from his past; on the contrary, he tried to make amends by building orphanages and helping society. Amir observes that he himself has done just the opposite: he has simply taken his shame out upon the same people he had already hurt. Only by righting his past can he atone for his sins; oblivion will accomplish nothing. And so Amir sets off to Afghanistan, a journey that Geraldine Pearson describes as "a way for Amir to deal with his own guilt about Hassan and ultimately forms a story of redemption and resolution" (66). He returns not only to end his own denial and guilt and atone for his sins, but also for the sins of his father. His father committed the offense that brought Hassan into the world. Rescuing Hassan's son, Sohrab, will bring a resolution to this problem that his father started and that Amir has exacerbated. Amir is determined to at last deal with his past and sets off for Afghanistan, resolving to make good out of bad.

Subsequently, his new knowledge and determination to correct his wrongs give him newfound strength, both physically and mentally. Later, as Amir's teeth break, ribs snap, and skin tears from Assef's vicious thrashing, Amir oddly feels serenely calm:

"I felt at peace. . . . My body was broken . . . but I felt healed. Healed at last" (Hosseini 289). Amir does not mind Assef's blows because to him they are weak compared to the personal fulfillment he found when redeeming himself by saving Sohrab. He knows that now he, just like his father, has done an act of service to help right his past wrongs. The blows of Assef pale in comparison to the weight of decades of shame, guilt, and lies lifted from Amir's shoulders. Likewise, after Amir brings Sohrab to America, and Sohrab gives a small, barely perceptible smile, Amir runs "with the wind blowing in my face, and a smile as wide as the Valley of Panjsher on my lips" (Hosseini 371). Although seemingly insignificant, Sohrab's smile to Amir represents a new beginning. For the first time in a long time, Sohrab smiles—something that he would never have done voluntarily in Assef's sexual slavery in Afghanistan. His first smile also symbolizes Amir's spiritual renewal through ridding his soul of his long-past sins. For the first time since Hassan's rape on that cold winter day in 1975, Amir's conscience is clean and he is truly happy.

However, Amir's newfound happiness comes only after much determination and bravery. Only after mustering courage to deal with his childhood past and committing himself toward redressing his wrongs is he able to achieve it. However, his successful transformation in character also brings Hosseini's work into a larger context and forces a look at society itself. The novel calls upon the reader to honestly face his own past and overcome any of his own wrongs by striving towards goodness and grace. As Amir's story demonstrates, these personal challenges can be conquered through conscious thought and determination. And though he is only one person in the novel who found a way to fulfillment and salvation, Amir can count himself among those who successfully free themselves from shame and finally find a path to true happiness.

Works Cited

Algoo-Baksh, Stella. "Ghosts of the Past." Canadian Literature 184 (Spring 2005): 143. Academic Search Complete. Ebsco. Kingwood HS Lib., Kingwood. 9 April 2008 <http://web.ebscohost.com>.

Hosseini, Khaled. The Kite Runner. New York: Riverhead Books, 2003.

"Khaled Hosseini." Contemporary Authors Online. Thomson Gale. Kingwood HS Lib., Kingwood. 9 April 2008 <http://galenet.galegroup.com>.

Morace, Robert. "The Kite Runner." Magill's Literary Annual 2004. Salem Press, 2004. Literary Reference Center. Ebsco. Kingwood HS Lib., Kingwood. 9 April 2008 <http://web.ebscohost.com>.

Pearson, Geraldine. "Book Review." Journal of Child & Adolescent Psychiatric Nursing 20.1 (Feb 2007): 66. Academic Search Complete. Ebsco. Kingwood HS Lib., Kingwood. 9 April 2008 <http://web.ebscohost.com>.

Quiz 1

1. **From what year does Amir narrate the story?**
   A. 2002.
   B. 2007.
   C. 1975.
   D. 1996.

2. **What does Rahim Khan say to Amir over the phone?**
   A. "The harelipped kite runner."
   B. "There is a way to be good again."
   C. "For you, a thousand times over."
   D. "Let's go fly a kite."

3. **Which of the following did Baba NOT do?**
   A. Miss Hassan's birthday.
   B. Throw frequent dinner parties.
   C. Build an orphanage.
   D. Neglect Amir.

4. **How did Amir's mother die?**
   A. In childbirth.
   B. Of cancer.
   C. Peacefully, in her sleep.
   D. The Taliban shot her.

5. **What was Amir's mother's name?**
   A. Sohrab
   B. Sanaubar
   C. Sasa
   D. Sofia

6. **What was Amir's mother's profession?**
   A. Teacher.
   B. Servant.
   C. Novelist.
   D. Physician.

7. **What key concept distinguishes Sunni and Shi'a Islam?**
   A. Mosques.
   B. Praying towards Mecca.
   C. Muhammad.
   D. Caliphate.

8. **According to Ali, why did Amir and Hassan have a special kinship?**
   A. They were nursed by the same woman.
   B. They were the city's champion kite fighters.
   C. They were half-brothers.
   D. They both loved the story of Sohrab and Rostam.

9. **How were Amir and Hassan really related?**
   A. They were kite fighting opponents.
   B. They were schoolmates.
   C. They were both Baba's servants.
   D. They were half-brothers.

10. **How did Sanaubar treat Hassan when he was born?**
   A. She told him stories.
   B. She rejected him.
   C. She read him poems.
   D. She mourned for him.

11. **How were Ali and Sanaubar related?**
   A. Cousins.
   B. Spouses.
   C. Cousins and fellow professors.
   D. Cousins and Spouses.

12. **The term "Hazara" describes whom of the following?**
   A. Ali.
   B. Rahim Khan.
   C. Baba.
   D. Assef.

13. What does Amir call Assef in retrospect?

    A. A Hazara.

    B. A harelipped kite runner.

    C. A sociopath.

    D. A true Afghan.

14. What was Amir's first word?

    A. "Hassan."

    B. "Baba."

    C. "Sasa."

    D. "Amir."

15. What was Hassan's first word?

    A. "Ali."

    B. "Amir."

    C. "Book."

    D. "Kite."

16. How did Amir learn about Hazara history?

    A. Assef told him.

    B. He secretly read a book.

    C. A mullah told him.

    D. Baba told him.

17. What is another term for a harelip?

    A. A pomegranate.

    B. A warrior.

    C. A cleft lip.

    D. A mule's lip.

18. Baba was rumored to have done what?

    A. Married twice.

    B. Built a school.

    C. Wrestled a bear.

    D. Slept with Sanaubar.

19. **What is Baba's opinion of the fundamentally religious?**
    A. He does not care one way or the other.
    B. He thinks they are gods.
    C. He thinks they are crazy.
    D. He thinks they should die.

20. **According to Baba, what is the greatest sin?**
    A. Cheating.
    B. Drinking.
    C. Stealing.
    D. Lying.

21. **For what did Amir feel Baba blamed him?**
    A. The corn dying.
    B. His mother's death.
    C. Assef's bad behavior.
    D. Hassan's illiteracy.

22. **As a child, Amir was talented at what?**
    A. Soccer.
    B. Fighting.
    C. Buzkashi.
    D. Reciting poetry.

23. **Whom did Baba see in the bleachers at the Buzkashi game?**
    A. Mohammad Daoud.
    B. Henry Kissinger.
    C. Zahir Shah.
    D. Ronald Reagan.

24. **Who said, "If I hadn't seen the doctor pull him out of my wife with my own eyes, I'd never believe he's my son."**
    A. Hassan.
    B. Ali.
    C. Rahim Khan.
    D. Baba.

25. **How did Ali become an orphan?**
    A. The Taliban killed his parents.
    B. His parents died in an accident.
    C. His parents committed suicide.
    D. Al Qaeda killed his parents.

Quiz 1 Answer Key

1. **(A)** 2002.
2. **(B)** "There is a way to be good again."
3. **(A)** Miss Hassan's birthday.
4. **(A)** In childbirth.
5. **(D)** Sofia
6. **(A)** Teacher.
7. **(D)** Caliphate.
8. **(A)** They were nursed by the same woman.
9. **(D)** They were half-brothers.
10. **(B)** She rejected him.
11. **(D)** Cousins and Spouses.
12. **(A)** Ali.
13. **(C)** A sociopath.
14. **(B)** "Baba."
15. **(B)** "Amir."
16. **(B)** He secretly read a book.
17. **(C)** A cleft lip.
18. **(C)** Wrestled a bear.
19. **(C)** He thinks they are crazy.
20. **(C)** Stealing.
21. **(B)** His mother's death.
22. **(D)** Reciting poetry.
23. **(B)** Henry Kissinger.
24. **(D)** Baba.
25. **(B)** His parents died in an accident.

Quiz 2

1. **Who is "the face of Afghanistan" to Amir?**
    A. Hassan.
    B. Sohrab.
    C. Rahim Khan.
    D. Baba.

2. **What was the distinguishing feature of Amir's first story?**
    A. Alliteration.
    B. Metaphor.
    C. Rhyme.
    D. Irony.

3. **What did Hassan point out in Amir's story?**
    A. A spelling error.
    B. A plot hole.
    C. A lie.
    D. Irony.

4. **What happened on July 17, 1973?**
    A. The Taliban rolled into Kabul.
    B. A military coup.
    C. Amir and Baba fled Afghanistan.
    D. The Soviets invaded Kabul.

5. **Who was Assef's idol?**
    A. Hitler.
    B. Osama bin Laden.
    C. Saddam Hussein.
    D. Mussolini.

6. **What was Assef's favorite weapon?**
    A. A stone.
    B. Brass knuckles.
    C. A slingshot.
    D. A knife.

7. **How did Hassan make Assef back down?**
    A. By telling on him.
    B. By insulting him.
    C. By throwing a stone at him.
    D. By aiming his slingshot at his eye.

8. **How did Hassan's harelip get fixed?**
    A. Baba gave him the surgery for his birthday.
    B. A doctor in Pakistan fixed it.
    C. Amir inisted that Baba pay for it.
    D. It did not get fixed.

9. **In what season did the boys go kite fighting?**
    A. Spring.
    B. Winter.
    C. Summer.
    D. Fall.

10. **What coated the kite strings in kite fighting?**
    A. Rubber.
    B. Tar.
    C. Metal.
    D. Glass.

11. **What else happened during this season?**
    A. The schools were closed.
    B. A festival.
    C. The women danced in the streets.
    D. The men went fishing.

12. **What made Hassan such a good kite runner?**
    A. An innate sense of where the kite would land.
    B. Years of careful study.
    C. A secret mirror that let him see the kite without looking up.
    D. A genetic predisposition.

13. **What did Amir promise to buy Hassan when they grew up?**
    A. A bicycle.
    B. A Mustang.
    C. A microwave.
    D. A television.

14. **Who said, "I like where I live?"**
    A. Hassan.
    B. Amir.
    C. Kamal.
    D. Assef.

15. **What did Assef do to Hassan?**
    A. He stole his kite.
    B. He beat him.
    C. He raped him.
    D. He gave him a harelip.

16. **What did Amir do to help Hassan?**
    A. Nothing.
    B. He took the kite.
    C. He ran and got Ali.
    D. He threatened Assef with his slingshot.

17. **According to Amir, what is "the look of the lamb?"**
    A. A look of defeat.
    B. A look of despair.
    C. A look of defiance.
    D. A look of pleading.

18. **Who had "the look of the lamb?"**
    A. Hassan.
    B. Assef's friends.
    C. Amir.
    D. Assef.

19. **How did Amir deal with his guilt?**
    A. He avoided Hassan.
    B. He told Rahim Khan what happened.
    C. He wrote a story about it.
    D. He told Ali about it.

20. **What embarrassing ailment does Amir have?**
    A. Asthma.
    B. Flatulence.
    C. Carsickness.
    D. Eczema.

21. **What did Baba do when Amir suggested getting new servants?**
    A. Fixed Hassan's harelip.
    B. Bought Hassan a new bike.
    C. Pretended he did not hear.
    D. Threatened to strike Amir.

22. **What did Hassan refuse to do for Amir?**
    A. Learn how to read.
    B. His chores.
    C. Sleep in the house.
    D. Hit him with a pomegranate.

23. **What was the only birthday present Amir could bear to use?**
    A. The notebook from Rahim Khan.
    B. The wristwatch from Baba.
    C. The book from Assef.
    D. The book from Ali and Hassan.

24. **How did Hassan respond to Amir's accusations of theft?**
    A. He said nothing.
    B. He admitted to stealing.
    C. He tried to kill himself.
    D. He called Amir out as a liar.

25. **What happened for the first time after Hassan and Ali left?**
    A. It rained.
    B. Baba cried.
    C. There was an earthquake.
    D. Baba hit Amir.

Quiz 2 Answer Key

1. **(A)** Hassan.
2. **(D)** Irony.
3. **(B)** A plot hole.
4. **(B)** A military coup.
5. **(A)** Hitler.
6. **(B)** Brass knuckles.
7. **(D)** By aiming his slingshot at his eye.
8. **(A)** Baba gave him the surgery for his birthday.
9. **(B)** Winter.
10. **(D)** Glass.
11. **(A)** The schools were closed.
12. **(A)** An innate sense of where the kite would land.
13. **(D)** A television.
14. **(A)** Hassan.
15. **(C)** He raped him.
16. **(A)** Nothing.
17. **(A)** A look of defeat.
18. **(A)** Hassan.
19. **(A)** He avoided Hassan.
20. **(C)** Carsickness.
21. **(D)** Threatened to strike Amir.
22. **(D)** Hit him with a pomegranate.
23. **(A)** The notebook from Rahim Khan.
24. **(B)** He admitted to stealing.
25. **(B)** Baba cried.

Quiz 3

1. **What do Afghans call the Soviets?**
    A. Talibs.
    B. Mullahs.
    C. Shorawi.
    D. Mujahedin.

2. **Why did Kamal's father shoot himself?**
    A. In order to save Kamal.
    B. Because Kamal had died.
    C. In order to save his wife.
    D. It was an accident.

3. **What did Mr. Nguyen say that offended Baba?**
    A. He called him a Muslim.
    B. He called him an Afghan.
    C. He asked for his ID.
    D. He praised the Soviet Union.

4. **Where did Baba work in California?**
    A. A garage.
    B. A restaurant kitchen.
    C. A bar.
    D. A gas station.

5. **What did Baba say the night of Amir's graduation?**
    A. That he had been lying to Amir.
    B. That he loved the idea of America.
    C. That he wanted to go back to Kabul.
    D. That he wished Hassan were there.

6. **Why did Amir call Soraya his "Swap Meet Princess?"**
    A. He did not call her that.
    B. She had a T-shirt that said that.
    C. It was the same thing Baba called Amir's mother.
    D. They met at the flea market.

7. **What did General Taheri do for work in America?**
    A. He did not work.
    B. He sold hot dogs.
    C. He ran a convenience store.
    D. He worked in a garage.

8. **What did Baba refuse?**
    A. To ask for Soraya's hand.
    B. Palliative cancer treatment.
    C. To return to Afghanistan to die.
    D. Alcohol, at all times.

9. **What happened to Khanum Taheri during the time Soraya had run off?**
    A. She had a stroke.
    B. She learned how to read.
    C. She adopted a second child.
    D. She lost her mother.

10. **What did Amir find out about Soraya the night they were engaged?**
    A. That she was infertile.
    B. That she was not a virgin.
    C. That she did not believe in Islam.
    D. That she was a Hazara.

11. **What is it called when a man's father proposes to a woman on his son's behalf?**
    A. awroussi.
    B. lafz.
    C. khastegari.
    D. watan.

12. **Why do Amir and Soraya skip their engagement party?**
    A. Because they are infertile.
    B. Because Baba is dying.
    C. Because they do not like to follow tradition.
    D. Because they do not like pomp and circumstance.

13. **What did Amir find out that made him cry?**
    A. Baba knew about Hassan's rape.
    B. Baba asked Soraya to read him Amir's stories.
    C. Sofia Akrami was not his real mother.
    D. Baba told Soraya that he loved Hassan.

14. **What did General Taheri forbid Khanum Taheri to do?**
    A. Sing.
    B. Work.
    C. Eat dessert.
    D. Dance.

15. **What word describes Khanum Taheri?**
    A. gossip.
    B. traitor.
    C. hypochondriac.
    D. battered woman.

16. **Why did Amir pity Soraya sometimes?**
    A. Because she did not know how to read.
    B. Because her parents did not really love her.
    C. Because she never found out she had a brother.
    D. Because she was subject to a sexual double standard.

17. **What was the cause of Amir and Soraya's infertility?**
    A. It was unexplainable.
    B. They did not like to make love.
    C. Soraya was not producing eggs.
    D. Amir had a low sperm count.

18. **What did General Taheri discourage the couple from doing?**
    A. Praying.
    B. Adopting.
    C. Consulting fertility specialists.
    D. Moving back to Kabul.

19. **Where did Amir fly to see Rahim Khan?**
    A. Mazar-i-Sharif.
    B. Peshawar.
    C. Jalalabad.
    D. Islamabad.

20. **What didn't Rahim Khan remember?**
    A. Amir's name.
    B. Baba's secret.
    C. Hassan's rape.
    D. The notebook.

21. **Why did Rahim Khan seek out Hassan?**
    A. He felt lonely and weak.
    B. He promised Baba he would do so.
    C. He wanted to tell him Baba's secret.
    D. He was afraid of the Taliban.

22. **What was Hassan's wife's name?**
    A. Soraya.
    B. Farzana.
    C. Sanaubar.
    D. Sofia.

23. **How did Hassan mourn Baba?**
    A. He wore black for forty days.
    B. He planted corn.
    C. He did not mourn Baba.
    D. He painted the house.

24. **What happened to Hassan's daughter?**
    A. He never had a daughter.
    B. She was stillborn.
    C. She ran away.
    D. She died at the hands of the Taliban.

25. **After whom did Hassan name Sohrab?**
   A. His favorite legendary hero.
   B. The former king.
   C. Ali's father.
   D. Baba's father.

Quiz 3 Answer Key

1. **(C)** Shorawi.
2. **(B)** Because Kamal had died.
3. **(C)** He asked for his ID.
4. **(D)** A gas station.
5. **(D)** That he wished Hassan were there.
6. **(D)** They met at the flea market.
7. **(A)** He did not work.
8. **(B)** Palliative cancer treatment.
9. **(A)** She had a stroke.
10. **(B)** That she was not a virgin.
11. **(C)** khastegari.
12. **(B)** Because Baba is dying.
13. **(B)** Baba asked Soraya to read him Amir's stories.
14. **(A)** Sing.
15. **(C)** hypochondriac.
16. **(D)** Because she was subject to a sexual double standard.
17. **(A)** It was unexplainable.
18. **(B)** Adopting.
19. **(B)** Peshawar.
20. **(D)** The notebook.
21. **(A)** He felt lonely and weak.
22. **(B)** Farzana.
23. **(A)** He wore black for forty days.
24. **(B)** She was stillborn.
25. **(A)** His favorite legendary hero.

Quiz 4

1. **What did Hassan NOT teach Sohrab how to do?**
   A. Read.
   B. Shoot a slingshot.
   C. Drink.
   D. Write.

2. **Why did Sanaubar return?**
   A. To find Rahim Khan.
   B. To deliver Sohrab.
   C. To make peace with Hassan.
   D. To get medical help.

3. **How did Hassan die?**
   A. Defending Baba's house.
   B. In a riot.
   C. In Ghazi Stadium.
   D. No one knows.

4. **Who was held accountable for Hassan and Farzana's deaths?**
   A. The Hazara people.
   B. The Taliban.
   C. No one.
   D. The PDPA.

5. **Why is Farid rude to Amir?**
   A. Because Amir went to America.
   B. Because he gets car sick.
   C. Because Amir does not have a beard.
   D. Because he dislikes Sunnis.

6. **Who calls Amir "a true Afghan?"**
   A. Rahim Khan.
   B. Farid.
   C. Wahid.
   D. Assef.

7. **Where is the orphanage where Sohrab was staying?**
     A. Mazar-i-Sharif.
     B. Wazir Akbar Khan.
     C. Peshawar.
     D. Karteh-Seh.

8. **Who are the Caldwells?**
     A. An American couple who flee Afghanistan just before Amir arrives.
     B. The former royal family of Afghanistan.
     C. An American couple Rahim Khan fabricates.
     D. The owners of the convenience store in Fremont.

9. **What does Amir leave under Wahid's mattress?**
     A. American clothes.
     B. Money.
     C. His notebook.
     D. A wristwatch.

10. **What does Amir have to wear to disguise himself?**
     A. A burqa.
     B. A fake beard.
     C. A long braid.
     D. Sunglasses.

11. **What was Baba's sin?**
     A. Betraying Hassan.
     B. Shaming Ali.
     C. Killing a man.
     D. Disgracing a mosque.

12. **How did Amir and Farid bond at the hotel?**
     A. By sharing food.
     B. By flying kites.
     C. By telling jokes.
     D. By fighting.

13. **What was the alleged crime of those murdered at Ghazi Stadium?**
    A. Dancing.
    B. Talking Loudly.
    C. Stealing.
    D. Adultery.

14. **What did Assef consider a message from God?**
    A. Hitler's death.
    B. His serving time in jail.
    C. The passing of his kidney stone.
    D. His parents' success in Australia.

15. **What did Assef make Sohrab wear?**
    A. Makeup.
    B. Nothing at all.
    C. A bedsheet.
    D. High heels.

16. **How did Sohrab injure Assef?**
    A. He split his lip.
    B. He broke his ribs.
    C. He put out his eye.
    D. He broke his orbital bone.

17. **Why did Sohrab run off in Islamabad?**
    A. To look at the mosque.
    B. To get food.
    C. To find his parents.
    D. To escape from Assef.

18. **What did the key Rahim Khan left Amir open?**
    A. A safety deposit box.
    B. His apartment.
    C. Nothing--the key was symbolic.
    D. A car.

19. **What was Raymond Andrews advice?**
    A. To bribe the INS.
    B. To put Sohrab in an orphanage temporarily.
    C. To give up.
    D. To live in Pakistan.

20. **What did Omar Faisal tell Amir?**
    A. That he knew Baba.
    B. To give up.
    C. That he admired him.
    D. That he despised him.

21. **Who managed to get Sohrab a visa?**
    A. Sharif.
    B. General Taheri.
    C. Sanaubar.
    D. Amir.

22. **Why did Sohrab try to kill himself?**
    A. He believed God wanted him to.
    B. He did not want to go to an orphanage.
    C. He was a sociopath.
    D. He did not; it was an accident.

23. **What did Amir do in the hospital for the first time in fifteen years?**
    A. Drink alcohol.
    B. Wish he was not an Afghan.
    C. Curse Baba.
    D. Pray.

24. **What did Sohrab refuse to do in America?**
    A. Leave the house.
    B. Eat.
    C. Speak.
    D. Sleep.

25. **What did Amir tell General Taheri never to call Sohrab?**
   A. A Shiite.
   B. An Afghan.
   C. A Hazara boy.
   D. A Sunni.

Quiz 4 Answer Key

1. **(C)** Drink.
2. **(C)** To make peace with Hassan.
3. **(A)** Defending Baba's house.
4. **(C)** No one.
5. **(A)** Because Amir went to America.
6. **(C)** Wahid.
7. **(D)** Karteh-Seh.
8. **(C)** An American couple Rahim Khan fabricates.
9. **(B)** Money.
10. **(B)** A fake beard.
11. **(B)** Shaming Ali.
12. **(C)** By telling jokes.
13. **(D)** Adultery.
14. **(C)** The passing of his kidney stone.
15. **(A)** Makeup.
16. **(C)** He put out his eye.
17. **(A)** To look at the mosque.
18. **(A)** A safety deposit box.
19. **(C)** To give up.
20. **(C)** That he admired him.
21. **(A)** Sharif.
22. **(B)** He did not want to go to an orphanage.
23. **(D)** Pray.
24. **(C)** Speak.
25. **(C)** A Hazara boy.

Quiz 5

1. **What does Amir do for Sohrab at the end?**
    A. Takes him to therapy.
    B. Helps him make a friend.
    C. Runs a kite for him.
    D. Embraces him.

2. **What does Amir tell Sohrab?**
    A. "We both got what we deserved."
    B. "There is a way to be good again."
    C. "For you, a thousand times over."
    D. "You are my son."

3. **What are the last words of the novel?**
    A. "There is a way to be good again."
    B. "For you, a thousand times over."
    C. "I was home."
    D. "I ran."

Quiz 5 Answer Key

1. **(C)** Runs a kite for him.
2. **(C)** "For you, a thousand times over."
3. **(D)** "I ran."

ClassicNotes

GrAdeSaver™

Getting you the grade since 1999™

Other ClassicNotes from GradeSaver™

1984
Absalom, Absalom
Adam Bede
The Adventures of Augie
   March
The Adventures of
   Huckleberry Finn
The Adventures of Tom
   Sawyer
The Aeneid
Agamemnon
The Age of Innocence
The Alchemist (Coelho)
The Alchemist (Jonson)
Alice in Wonderland
All My Sons
All Quiet on the Western
   Front
All the King's Men
All the Pretty Horses
Allen Ginsberg's Poetry
The Ambassadors
American Beauty
And Then There Were
   None
Angela's Ashes
Animal Farm
Anna Karenina
Anthem
Antigone
Antony and Cleopatra
Aristotle's Ethics
Aristotle's Poetics
Aristotle's Politics
As I Lay Dying
As You Like It

Astrophil and Stella
Atlas Shrugged
Atonement
The Awakening
Babbitt
The Bacchae
Bartleby the Scrivener
The Bean Trees
The Bell Jar
Beloved
Benito Cereno
Beowulf
Bhagavad-Gita
Billy Budd
Black Boy
Bleak House
Bless Me, Ultima
Blindness
Blood Wedding
The Bloody Chamber
Bluest Eye
The Bonfire of the
   Vanities
The Book of the Duchess
   and Other Poems
The Book Thief
Brave New World
Breakfast at Tiffany's
Breakfast of Champions
The Brief Wondrous Life
   of Oscar Wao
The Brothers Karamazov
The Burning Plain and
   Other Stories
A Burnt-Out Case
By Night in Chile

Call of the Wild
Candide
The Canterbury Tales
Cat on a Hot Tin Roof
Cat's Cradle
Catch-22
The Catcher in the Rye
The Caucasian Chalk
   Circle
Charlotte Temple
Charlotte's Web
The Cherry Orchard
The Chocolate War
The Chosen
A Christmas Carol
Christopher Marlowe's
   Poems
Chronicle of a Death
   Foretold
Civil Disobedience
Civilization and Its
   Discontents
A Clockwork Orange
Coleridge's Poems
The Color of Water
The Color Purple
Comedy of Errors
Communist Manifesto
A Confederacy of
   Dunces
Confessions
Connecticut Yankee in
   King Arthur's Court
The Consolation of
   Philosophy
Coriolanus

For our full list of over 250 Study Guides, Quizzes,
Sample College Application Essays, Literature Essays and E-texts, visit:

www.gradesaver.com

ClassicNotes

GradeSaver™

Getting you the grade since 1999™

Other ClassicNotes from GradeSaver™

The Count of Monte Cristo
The Country Wife
Crime and Punishment
The Crucible
Cry, the Beloved Country
The Crying of Lot 49
The Curious Incident of the Dog in the Night-time
Cymbeline
Daisy Miller
David Copperfield
Death in Venice
Death of a Salesman
The Death of Ivan Ilych
Democracy in America
Devil in a Blue Dress
Dharma Bums
The Diary of a Young Girl by Anne Frank
Disgrace
Divine Comedy-I: Inferno
Do Androids Dream of Electric Sheep?
Doctor Faustus (Marlowe)
A Doll's House
Don Quixote Book I
Don Quixote Book II
Dora: An Analysis of a Case of Hysteria
Dr. Jekyll and Mr. Hyde
Dracula

Dubliners
East of Eden
Electra by Sophocles
The Electric Kool-Aid Acid Test
Emily Dickinson's Collected Poems
Emma
Ender's Game
Endgame
The English Patient
The Epic of Gilgamesh
Ethan Frome
The Eumenides
Everyman: Morality Play
Everything is Illuminated
The Faerie Queene
Fahrenheit 451
The Fall of the House of Usher
A Farewell to Arms
The Federalist Papers
Fences
Flags of Our Fathers
Flannery O'Connor's Stories
For Whom the Bell Tolls
The Fountainhead
Frankenstein
Franny and Zooey
The Giver
The Glass Castle
The Glass Menagerie
The God of Small Things
Goethe's Faust
The Good Earth

The Good Woman of Setzuan
The Grapes of Wrath
Great Expectations
The Great Gatsby
Grendel
The Guest
Gulliver's Travels
Hamlet
The Handmaid's Tale
Hard Times
Haroun and the Sea of Stories
Harry Potter and the Philosopher's Stone
Heart of Darkness
Hedda Gabler
Henry IV (Pirandello)
Henry IV Part 1
Henry IV Part 2
Henry V
Herzog
Hippolytus
The Hobbit
Homo Faber
House of Mirth
The House of the Seven Gables
The House of the Spirits
House on Mango Street
How the Garcia Girls Lost Their Accents
Howards End
A Hunger Artist
I Know Why the Caged Bird Sings

For our full list of over 250 Study Guides, Quizzes,
Sample College Application Essays, Literature Essays and E-texts, visit:

www.gradesaver.com

ClassicNotes

GradeSaver™

Getting you the grade since 1999™

Other ClassicNotes from GradeSaver™

I, Claudius
An Ideal Husband
Iliad
The Importance of Being
   Earnest
In Cold Blood
In Our Time
In the Time of the
   Butterflies
Inherit the Wind
An Inspector Calls
Into the Wild
Invisible Man
The Island of Dr. Moreau
Jane Eyre
Jazz
The Jew of Malta
Joseph Andrews
The Joy Luck Club
Julius Caesar
The Jungle
Jungle of Cities
Kama Sutra
Kate Chopin's Short
   Stories
Kidnapped
King Lear
King Solomon's Mines
The Kite Runner
Last of the Mohicans
Leaves of Grass
The Legend of Sleepy
   Hollow
A Lesson Before Dying
Leviathan
Libation Bearers

Life is Beautiful
Life of Pi
Light In August
Like Water for Chocolate
The Lion, the Witch and
   the Wardrobe
Little Women
Lolita
Long Day's Journey Into
   Night
Look Back in Anger
Lord Jim
Lord of the Flies
The Lord of the Rings:
   The Fellowship of the
   Ring
The Lord of the Rings:
   The Return of the
   King
The Lord of the Rings:
   The Two Towers
A Lost Lady
The Lottery and Other
   Stories
Love in the Time of
   Cholera
The Love Song of J.
   Alfred Prufrock
The Lovely Bones
Lucy
Macbeth
Madame Bovary
Maggie: A Girl of the
   Streets and Other
   Stories
Manhattan Transfer

Mankind: Medieval
   Morality Plays
Mansfield Park
The Marrow of Tradition
The Master and
   Margarita
MAUS
The Mayor of
   Casterbridge
Measure for Measure
Medea
Merchant of Venice
Metamorphoses
The Metamorphosis
Middlemarch
A Midsummer Night's
   Dream
Moby Dick
A Modest Proposal and
   Other Satires
Moll Flanders
Mother Courage and Her
   Children
Mrs. Dalloway
Much Ado About
   Nothing
My Antonia
Mythology
The Namesake
Native Son
Nickel and Dimed: On
   (Not) Getting By in
   America
Night
Nine Stories
No Exit

For our full list of over 250 Study Guides, Quizzes,
Sample College Application Essays, Literature Essays and E-texts, visit:

www.gradesaver.com

ClassicNotes

GradeSaver™

Getting you the grade since 1999™

Other ClassicNotes from GradeSaver™

Northanger Abbey
Notes from Underground
O Pioneers
The Odyssey
Oedipus Rex or Oedipus
   the King
Of Mice and Men
The Old Man and the Sea
Oliver Twist
On Liberty
On the Road
One Day in the Life of
   Ivan Denisovich
One Flew Over the
   Cuckoo's Nest
One Hundred Years of
   Solitude
Oroonoko
Oryx and Crake
Othello
Our Town
The Outsiders
Pale Fire
Pamela: Or Virtue
   Rewarded
Paradise Lost
A Passage to India
The Pearl
Percy Shelley: Poems
Perfume: The Story of a
   Murderer
Persepolis: The Story of
   a Childhood
Persuasion
Phaedra
Phaedrus

The Piano Lesson
The Picture of Dorian
   Gray
Poe's Poetry
Poe's Short Stories
Poems of W.B. Yeats:
   The Rose
Poems of W.B. Yeats:
   The Tower
The Poems of William
   Blake
The Poetry of Robert
   Frost
The Poisonwood Bible
Pope's Poems and Prose
Portrait of the Artist as a
   Young Man
Pride and Prejudice
The Prince
The Professor's House
Prometheus Bound
Pudd'nhead Wilson
Pygmalion
Rabbit, Run
A Raisin in the Sun
The Real Life of
   Sebastian Knight
Rebecca
The Red Badge of
   Courage
The Remains of the Day
The Republic
Rhinoceros
Richard II
Richard III

The Rime of the Ancient
   Mariner
Rip Van Winkle and
   Other Stories
The Road
Robinson Crusoe
Roll of Thunder, Hear
   My Cry
Romeo and Juliet
A Room of One's Own
A Room With a View
A Rose For Emily and
   Other Short Stories
Rosencrantz and
   Guildenstern Are
   Dead
Salome
The Scarlet Letter
The Scarlet Pimpernel
The Seagull
Season of Migration to
   the North
Second Treatise of
   Government
The Secret Life of Bees
The Secret River
Secret Sharer
Sense and Sensibility
A Separate Peace
Shakespeare's Sonnets
Shantaram
Short Stories of Ernest
   Hemingway
Short Stories of F. Scott
   Fitzgerald
Siddhartha

For our full list of over 250 Study Guides, Quizzes,
Sample College Application Essays, Literature Essays and E-texts, visit:

www.gradesaver.com

ClassicNotes

GradeSaver™

Getting you the grade since 1999™

Other ClassicNotes from GradeSaver™

Silas Marner
Sir Gawain and the
   Green Knight
Sister Carrie
Six Characters in Search
   of an Author
Slaughterhouse Five
Snow Falling on Cedars
The Social Contract
Something Wicked This
   Way Comes
Song of Roland
Song of Solomon
Songs of Innocence and
   of Experience
Sons and Lovers
The Sorrows of Young
   Werther
The Sound and the Fury
The Spanish Tragedy
Spenser's Amoretti and
   Epithalamion
Spring Awakening
The Stranger
A Streetcar Named
   Desire
Sula
The Sun Also Rises
Tale of Two Cities
The Taming of the Shrew
The Tempest
Tender is the Night
Tess of the D'Urbervilles
Their Eyes Were
   Watching God
Things Fall Apart

The Things They Carried
A Thousand Splendid
   Suns
The Threepenny Opera
Through the Looking
   Glass
Thus Spoke Zarathustra
The Time Machine
Titus Andronicus
To Build a Fire
To Kill a Mockingbird
To the Lighthouse
The Tortilla Curtain
Touching Spirit Bear
Treasure Island
Trifles
Troilus and Cressida
Tropic of Cancer
Tropic of Capricorn
Tuesdays With Morrie
The Turn of the Screw
Twelfth Night
Twilight
Ulysses
Uncle Tom's Cabin
Utopia
Vanity Fair
A Very Old Man With
   Enormous Wings
Villette
The Visit
Volpone
Waiting for Godot
Waiting for Lefty
Walden
Washington Square

The Waste Land
The Wealth of Nations
Where the Red Fern
   Grows
White Fang
A White Heron and
   Other Stories
White Noise
White Teeth
Who's Afraid of Virginia
   Woolf
Wide Sargasso Sea
Wieland
Winesburg, Ohio
The Winter's Tale
The Woman Warrior
Wordsworth's Poetical
   Works
Woyzeck
A Wrinkle in Time
Wuthering Heights
The Yellow Wallpaper
Yonnondio: From the
   Thirties
Zeitoun

For our full list of over 250 Study Guides, Quizzes,
Sample College Application Essays, Literature Essays and E-texts, visit:

www.gradesaver.com